Clarity Spiral

The 4 Break-Thru Practices to Find the One Thing You're Called to Do

WILL MANCINI

Cover design and illustrations by James Bethany.
Interior design by Cory Hartman.

ISBN-10: 1790930029
ISBN-13: 9781790930029

This book is dedicated to the first thousand participants in the Younique Journey. These people undertook the task before the end of 2018 in either a weekly cohort or a Younique Accelerator—you know who you are. As homes and churches were opened in the early years of this grand project you opened your hearts and dreams. You became our inspiration in ways we could never anticipate. The Younique team learned more from you than we will ever learn as thousands upon thousands continue to walk the Clarity Spiral. May you continue to enjoy the view as you climb your personal Everest for God's glory.

CONTENTS

Part One

CALLED BY CALLING

Chapter 1

BACKSTORY

The Worst Way to Learn the Incredible Value of Personal Calling

"Calling is the truth that God calls us to himself so decisively that everything we are, everything we do, and everything we have is invested with a special devotion, dynamism, and direction lived out as a response to his summons and service."

–Os Guinness

This is a book about taking in the breathtaking vistas of audacious dreams. But I want to start at an unexpected place— the dark and narrow gorge of my life's greatest failure. After all, we all have high points and hard times on the journey.

One of my hardest was the first Christmas after the unraveling of my decade-long marriage. I was 33 years old with three kids—Jacob, Joel and Abby—who were nine, six, and three respectively. I moved out of my home and rented a two-bedroom apartment for the four of us. The second bedroom was really more of a big closet where the kids slept during their fifty-percent time with Dad. All three kids managed to fit into a bargain bunkbed—the kind made with flimsy, white metal tubing.

While walking this deep valley with my bewildered kids, the Christmas season heralded a "different kind of holiday" for my now-broken family. But I still wanted to make it memorable, so I started from scratch with decorations for the apartment. Sadly, my bank account was as empty as a Christmas tree bulb.

I found an artificial tree at Walmart with cool fiber-optic lights. The clearance section price was appealing, but I noticed that after five minutes of glittering fun, the high-tech tannenbaum would overheat and shut off. I convinced myself that it was no big deal: the kids could just blow on it until it cooled down and then hit the little reset switch.

I can still see the cash register that day ringing up the $72.56 price tag for the additional holiday paraphernalia. "Another purchase that I don't have the money for," I thought, swiping the credit card with one hand and brushing the tears off my cheek with the other so my kids wouldn't see. I think they had a decent Christmas that year, but I had never felt more lonely. I'm sure I devoured plenty of sweet holiday treats, but the taste I remember most is failure.

You and I have both experienced different levels of failure. But why would I start a book on personal calling with a snapshot from a deep valley of personal pain?

First, I want to testify to God's goodness. Although people let us down, the Lord has a knack for sticking around. He is always faithful, and a book on how to design your life would be a waste of time if I didn't start and end by giving all glory to Him.

Second, I am so optimistic about your life's call—even though we've never met—that as this book goes on you will be tempted to think I am a pie-in-the-sky guy. I want to blow your mind with your own potential, the capabilities you've not tuned into yet, but I can assure you that I don't have rose-colored glasses strapped to my face. I'm not afraid to call "bull" when I spot unfounded optimism. Unlike many writers and speakers in this category I use words like "dream" and "destiny" with precision; I approach life design as an engineer, not as an ice cream man.

After all, what is "life design" (or "life planning")? It is consciously deciding in advance how your life should look and function. It is laying the track for your activity by focused, intentional planning. It is discovering the highest and best use of your life for honoring God and helping others and then ordering your attention accordingly.

But third and most urgently, I don't want you to have to go through what I went through to learn what I learned about the power of your life's call.

How the Lesson of Calling Changed Me Forever

Before my deep valley experience, I was an ordained pastor enjoying ministry in a rapidly growing church. You could say I was a "called" man but I was not living from "calling." How do I know? Looking back, I see a man who always had something to prove and something to lose. I maneuvered people to make things happen. I sought the vocal affirmation of the people I taught. I grew jealous when coworkers thrived. Something was driving my vocational motivations. For me is was *not* a deepening awareness of my special assignment from God. It was a soul drift that sought approval and used a local church ministry context to find it.

> Looking back, I see a man who always had something to prove and something to lose.

I like the definition of "idol" that goes, "the thing you add to Jesus to make life work." Of course, the very nature of idolatry makes it hard to spot. Before my marital crisis, I didn't see my idolatry problem. I didn't know how heavily I was relying on being an all-American guy with a beautiful wife and picture-perfect kids as an up-and-coming pastor to make *my* life work.

But failure is an effective teacher. And the classroom of life's challenge schooled me in two ways.

First, the failure deepened my emotional connection to the gospel. I needed to know the person Jesus beyond the Sunday school categories and seminary-speak. "Savior and Lord" he had been. "Alpha and Omega" I had preached. But he would become more—a Friend. A delightful kind of friend who profoundly *liked* me and wanted to be *with* me just as he *made* me. Jesus came through—he stayed close to me and his love grew even sweeter.

Second, the failure challenged me to pursue what he put me on earth to do. Now that I was more secure as a human *being* and not just a human *doing,* I was free to find my calling. I was now prepared to get the *doing* part of life right. After all, God does makes humans to *do*: he commissioned us from the beginning to be fruitful, to multiply, to fill, to rule, to name, to serve, to generate life. I was ready to grab hold of that "commissioned sensibility." Some days, the raw, dry hope that God had made me to do *something*—even though it wasn't totally clear yet—was the only thing that got me out of bed in the morning.

Today I can testify to the awesome power of life calling. Despite a chapter in my life that included a subplot I didn't choose—bringing hurt, failure, and shame—the unfolding story of my life was being written. How so? It was being guided by God's dream for my life from before time. Yet at the same time, it was also being shaped by my proactive design. Each day through the mountains and valleys and even from the pit, a calling from God was present. The calling always starts with his initiative, as he alone is Maker and Caller; he alone is the ultimate Guide. Yet, that call moves from response to response and from grace to grace until it is known truly.

Eventually, if we pursue it, the reason that God put us on earth works its way into our life each day. For me, that calling over time became clear, specific, and articulated. It rooted me in very practical ways. It yielded a wonderful variety of fruit marking my life with optimism, hope, and vision. It grew *out of* disciplined self-awareness and *into* vocational risk-taking. It became vastly more precious to me than any artificial, manufactured image, including the one I had lost. My calling strengthened my identity, cultivated my confidence, powered my passion and directed my dreaming. It kept me going and it kept me growing even through one of my deepest valleys.

That was then. Now add fifteen years.

Each month gets better as a calling-conscious follower of Jesus. Today I live out my single life call through six different vocational "vehicles." I enjoy the autonomy, mastery, and euphoria of working in my sweet spot almost every minute of my day. I have a beautiful, supportive wife and four amazing children. Although I'm occasionally distracted by material things, I can honestly say that after my first job decision at 21, I've never made a vocational decision based primarily on money. Yet I have earned more than I ever planned for or even imagined.

Two Ways to Live

The benefits of living from a "Called Self" are enormous. But keep in mind that there is another way to live: living from a "False Self." As we'll see later, there are many influences that lead us away from being the persons God made us to be. In truth, it's easier to live from a False Self, but it doesn't *feel* easier. It comes naturally to live from False Self, but it doesn't *feel* natural. When we're not living from our Called Self, we know deep down that something isn't right—we know there's something more for us.

Given the slice of strife in my own backstory I want to speak hope into who you are today and where you are today. That's because the life calling that I discovered in and through my successes and failures is to make a life of more meaningful progress more accessible to every believer. God put me on earth to honor Him and serve others by "applying essence"—articulating what a person, team, or organization is made for at its core and putting that "One Thing" into action. You can think of this book as a manual for applying the essence of you: your Called Self, your Life Younique.

> The life calling that I discovered is to make a life of more meaningful progress more accessible to every believer.

You *can* discover the dream God has for *you*. And you can proactively design a powerful life; one that releases all of the potential God put inside of you.

You have too much talent to settle for a False Self. You can seize the substance of who God made you to be.

The world is too broken to live from a False Self. You can bring amazing value to the people around you.

Life is too enjoyable to endure a False Self. You can experience more meaning and blessing every day.

In the pages ahead, I'll show you how.

Chapter 2

PROBLEM

Why Solving This One Problem Will Solve Most Others in Your Life

"The two most important days of your life are the day you were born and the day you find out why."

—Mark Twain

I love reading a book that points out one big problem worth solving and takes me a long step toward the solution. I've written *The Clarity Spiral* to be that kind of book. The problem I want to address is this:

> *Even though each believer has a special calling from God, the vast majority never name it and so miss a huge opportunity to make a more meaningful contribution with their entire life.*

To better understand this problem, let's first do a survey of the word "calling." What exactly do we mean by "special calling from God"?

The Five Kinds of Calling

The word "calling" itself has five related yet distinct meanings.

Calling #1: Initiation of Communication or Summons

This is the most common use both in our day-to-day lives and in Scripture. We "call" one another on the phone. A mother "calls" the boy on the swing inside for dinner. In the narrative portions of Bible people are "calling" on one another in this sense on almost every page.

Calling #2: An Act of Naming

Like the first use of the term, this one is also used in today's culture and in Scripture. My daughter Abby "called" our dog Peeta. Or we might learn that a doctor "called" the procedure "optical coherence tomography." In Genesis we read that God "called" the light *day*, and the darkness he called *night*.

Calling #3: An Invitation to Relationship with God

This is a richly developed biblical concept. "Calling" in this sense can almost be used as a synonym for salvation.

It is used to define God's relationship to his people Israel in the Old Testament. For example, Deuteronomy 28:10 (ESV) reads, "And all the peoples of the earth shall see that you are **called** by the name of the LORD, and they shall be afraid of you." "Calling" in this passage captures the identity and love that God has for his distinct and chosen people, Israel.

A New Testament example of the term's use with regard to the new covenant (i.e., the new agreement between God and mankind) is Hebrews 9:15: "Therefore, he [Jesus] is the mediator of a new covenant, so that those who are *called* might receive the promise of the eternal inheritance, because a death has taken place for redemption from the transgressions committed under the first covenant."

Furthermore, the most common word to describe God's people today is the "church." The connotation of a "church building" is unfortunate, because the root meaning of the Greek word *ekklesia*, which our Bibles generally translate as "church," is literally the "called-out ones." God's people today are literally those who have been "called out" of the world in their identity as children of God and in their activity to join God's mission.

> God's people are literally those who have been "called out" of the world in their identity as children of God and in their activity to join God's mission.

Calling #4: A Metaphor for the Entire Life of Faith

If you scan the use of the term "calling" in the Bible, the idea encompasses the totality of following Jesus and living a Godward life beyond initial salvation. Take a look at a few passages from different New Testament books to glimpse the magnitude of "calling" in this broadest sense:

- "We know that all things work together for the good of those who love God, who are *called* according to his purpose" (Rom. 8:28).

- "For you were **called** to be free, brothers and sisters; only don't use this freedom as an opportunity for the flesh, but serve one another through love" (Gal. 5:13).

- "He has saved us and **called** us with a holy calling, not according to our works, but according to his own purpose and grace, which was given to us in Christ Jesus before time began" (2 Tim. 1:9).

- "But as the one who **called** you is holy, you also are to be holy in all your conduct" (1 Pet. 1:15).

In his classic work on the subject, *The Call*, Os Guinness concludes,

> In short, calling in the Bible is a central and dynamic theme that becomes a metaphor for the life of faith itself. To limit the word, as some insist, to a few texts and to a particular stage in salvation is to miss the forest for the trees. To be a disciple of Jesus is to be a "called one" and so to become "a follower of the Way."[1]

Over time, the "big" sense of this idea of calling has been referred to as "primary calling" or "common calling" because it is the same for all people.

The Younique Kind of Calling

We have now covered four significant ways the the term "calling" is used. The fifth definition of "calling" is the one we will use in this book.

Calling #5: Something That You Were Created to Do with Your Life

This use of the term gives rise to the vocabulary of "vocation," a word that comes from the Latin word *vocare,* which means "to call." The term "vocation" evolved through church history to refer to the nobility of work as someone's "summons from God." We are going to refer to this kind of calling as it pertains to your life as your "special calling" or your special assignment from God. (By the way, in this book I use a lot of terms interchangeably: "life's call," "personal calling," "One Thing," "Life Younique," "Called Self," and more besides. All of these refer to special calling.)

When I ask you throughout this book, "What were you created to do?" I am referring to this definition of calling. I am not asking the question, "What are you created to do that all other people do too?" That would refer to Callings #3 and #4: all people are called to God through faith in Jesus Christ. All people are called to live their lives in response and obedience to their Creator. All people are created to glorify God and serve others.

My co-inventor Dave Rhodes and I created a complete, one-of-a-kind system to help people discover their calling according to this fifth definition of calling. It's called Younique. Younique helps people answer these kinds of questions:

- What kind of work should I pursue with my life?

- How do I experience more vitality at my existing job?

- When do I need to make a vocational change?

- How will I measure the effectiveness of my life?

- What is my ultimate contribution to the world?

Now let's revisit the problem statement of this book: even though each believer has a special calling from God, the vast majority never name it and so miss a huge opportunity to make a more meaningful contribution with their entire life.

When I say that you have a special calling, I am suggesting that the trajectory of what you were created to do can be named. It can be explored, discussed, and prayed over. I can be clarified, codified, and celebrated. This is the secondary or special calling I am referring to.

Don't Misunderstand Me

Before moving on, let's make two very important distinctions.

Common Calling Is the Foundation and Context for Special Calling

All believers are called to honor God and help others all of the time. As Scripture teaches, "And whatever you do, in word or in deed, do everything in the name of the Lord Jesus, giving thanks to God the Father through him" (Col. 3:17). Jesus summarized the law masterfully with the singularity of love. To live life as a God-follower we are instructed to "love the Lord your God with all your heart, with all your soul, with all your strength, and with all your mind" and "your neighbor as yourself" (Luke 10:27). This is our *common calling* as Christians.

> I am asking your permission to move on from the subject of *common* calling to *special* calling.

Remember, I am not going to argue the case that every day of your life you should honor God and help others as many authors have done in countless books. That is not the purpose of this book, so I am asking your permission to move on from the subject of *common* calling to *special* calling.

Despite the foundational nature of common calling, the

question of special calling is of massive importance. For example, at the moment of writing this chapter, my first-born, Jacob, has graduated college (praise the Lord, Dad got a raise!) and my third-born, Abby, is about to enter college (easy come, easy go). The foundational importance of teaching my children how to follow Jesus cannot be overstated. But as a dad, I have the opportunity to guide their college preparation, work decisions, and career trajectory. What is the special calling of my children? That is a big question. What were they specially created to do?

Perspectives on Special Calling Have Been Abused through Church History

In both Catholic and Protestant traditions, leaders have historically made mistakes in how they thought and taught about special calling. The two biggest problems have been (1) to define full-time Christian work as a more "spiritual" kind of work and (2) to describe the discovery of special calling as a necessarily dramatic event or vivid experience in a person's life.

Is "Christian Work" More Valuable?

While both misrepresentations run rampant through all branches of the Christian family tree, the first is particularly harmful. Sadly, this misunderstanding is embedded in the English word "clergy," which comes from the Greek word for "call."

Full-time Christian work, like being a pastor or missionary, is a beautiful thing; I have experienced this personally. But it is not a "higher" calling, much less the only kind. God does not value full-time service in a church or parachurch setting more highly than every other way of serving one's neighbor. Pastoring is a noble call, but so is plumbing and police work.

Based on your spiritual heritage and faith background, you

may be reading with some "calling-colored glasses." You may still feel some guilt that you didn't sign up to work for the church (or, as Baptists like to say, to "surrender your life to the call of ministry"). Of course, if God calls you to that work, it's sin not to obey. But he doesn't call everyone to that, even though he calls everyone to *something*. Unfortunately, when I graduated with a chemical engineering degree from Penn State, my Christian influences made me feel like a second-class citizen if I didn't immediately become an overseas missionary. While pressure to go into a full-time ministry occupation is common, it's not healthy. *All* work is ministry. Every job can be engaged for the gospel to the glory of God.[2]

The Oscar-winning 1981 film *Chariots of Fire*, based on a true story, powerfully illustrates both this common misrepresentation of calling and a vibrant, full-orbed, God-honoring example of it.

In the 1920s, Eric Liddell, the son of Scottish missionaries to China, uses his prodigious athletic gifts to draw crowds in Scotland and preach the gospel to them. Yet his sister Jennie fears that sports have become a distraction that is tempting Liddell away from his true ministry calling. Her anxiety and criticism grow even sharper when Liddell, the United Kingdom's fastest sprinter, is invited to compete on Great Britain's Olympic team.

In a poignant moment on a hilltop, Liddell tells his sister that he has decided to return to China as a missionary (where he later died in a Japanese internment camp during World War II). Liddell's news that he would go to the mission field thrills Jennie with delight. But her brother insists that first he must compete. "I believe that God made me for a purpose—for China," he says. "But he also made me *fast*.

> What do you do that makes you feel the pleasure of God?

And when I run, *I feel his pleasure.* To give it up would be to hold him in contempt. . . . It's not just fun: to win is to honor him."

That's it! What do you do that makes you feel the pleasure of God? Whatever it is, whether operating formally in the church or not, you honor him by doing it . . . and by doing it *to win.* *That* is the special calling God dreamed for you. To give it up for someone else's idea of a higher calling is to hold God in contempt.

Is Special Calling Revealed Directly?

The second misrepresentation is the false notion that calling requires a vivid encounter with God or a special revelatory experience. The fact is that for some people the clarification of calling is dramatic and direct, but for most it's developed and discerned.

In Scripture we are given approximately 100 examples of people who heard God tell them in an upfront, unmistakable way to take on a certain job or career.[3] For example:

- God called Noah to build the ark.

- God used a burning bush to to redirect the vocation of Moses.

- God recruited Aaron and his sons to be priests.

- God raised up prophets like Samuel, Jeremiah, and Amos.

- God chose Abram and Sarah to a massive life relocation.

- God placed many in political leadership including Joseph, Saul, and David.

- God gifted Bezalel and Oholiab as master craftsmen.

- Jesus called a twelve-person core team that we know as the apostles.

- The Holy Spirit directed Barnabas and Saul to be the first Christian missionaries.

While these examples clarify that God can and does speak directly by various means—dreams, bushes, and angels, to name a few—Scripture's testimony is that most people do not "hear" God's call in a literal sense. Waiting for the Holy Spirit to text you is not one of the exercises in the Younique Vision Journey! The highly qualified team behind the Theology of Work Project contend, "If by 'calling' we mean a direct, unmistakable command from God to take up a particular task, job, profession or type of work, then calling is very rare in the Bible."[4]

> For some people the clarification of calling is dramatic and direct, but for most it's developed and discerned.

That leaves the rest of us to the good work of discerning and developing our calling. Perhaps God wants you to experience great joy in the discovery process or practice deeper dependence on him. Either way, there is a pathway. But the road of *less dramatic means* does not mean *less dramatic outcomes*, I can assure you.

Many Problems, One Solution

Imagine for a minute that you had crystal clarity on your special assignment from God. Dream about a dream job for just a moment. What do you think that would do to your energy level every day? How would that impact all of your relationships? How would your bank account be affected?

When it comes to money, allow me to whisper a little hint: when your call is clear you no longer feel nearly as strongly that you need more money to be happy. But simultaneously and ironically you are better equipped than ever to make more money. That is because living from passion and maximizing your abilities boosts the quality and the quantity of what you do and leads you to the places where it is valued most.

Hear me: I'm not saying that knowing your life's call solves *every* problem in life. But as I demonstrated from my own life in chapter 1, it can be an immense reservoir of comfort when those unsolvable problems strike. In addition, when you solve this one problem you really will solve many other problems in life, from vocational challenges to relational tensions to financial barriers. What I most want you to know is that God has issued a special call to you and only you. It's the only one you get, and you are the only one qualified to live it out. God wants you to become a professional at living the life he made you for.

The First Master Tool: The Clarity Spiral

This book covers four repeatable practices that guide the work of life design. These are essential. Leave one behind and the journey stops. Build them into your life and you will discover the daring adventure of living your special assignment from God.

To turn these fundamentals into footsteps, I have depicted them working together as a spiral. This figure helps us remember them more readily and share them with others more easily. But why a spiral?

Have you ever hiked up a steep mountain? You can't sprint in a straight line to the summit. You have to take a more indirect approach, walking by switchbacks or spiraling up until you reach the peak. The hike is longer that way, but it is less steep and more accessible.

When you picture the spiral, that's what I want you to capture in your mind's eye: a journey up your own personal Everest. Grasping your "One Thing"—your unique assignment

Ten Problems Solved by Knowing Your Calling

1) Do you feel stuck or stalled in your connection with God? Calling will refresh your intimacy with your Creator.

2) Do you wonder why bad things have happened to you? Calling can help unravel the mystery and infuse prior pain with present purpose.

3) Have you stopped dreaming like you did when you were a kid? Calling is an on-ramp to enjoying imagination again.

4) Do you want to make more money or live on less? Calling can right-size your relationship with finances.

5) Do you struggle with fear? Calling will grow your confidence and enable you to seize new opportunities.

6) Do you work too much? Calling will help you make healthier decisions because you separate "who you are" from "what you do."

7) Are you frustrated at work? Calling can jump-start motivation in your current job or re-map your vocational trajectory.

8) Are your relationships feeling shallow? Calling will guide you deeper.

9) Do you feel more tired these days? Calling will introduce replenishment to every area of your life.

10) Have you ever missed a New Year's resolution? Calling will help you focus your energy to accomplish bigger goals.

from God—is not something you can do immediately or directly. It takes years of spiraling—hiking slowly up the mountain of your life with ever-increasing perspective.

And here's a hint: as long as you are breathing there is always more perspective. That's why I encourage you to start and *never stop* discovering your personal calling. While I have enjoyed fantastic views on the way up my personal Everest, there is still a lot I can't see. And I can't wait to learn what's next. I like the way Maria Popova captured this idea when she said that life is a continual process of arrival into who we are.

Because of this, it's important that I clarify the relationship between the Clarity Spiral and Younique. As I said above, Younique is a one-of-a-kind system that Dave Rhodes and I created to help people discover their special calling from God. Through the Younique process, a person can achieve *break-thru clarity*—my term for accurate, articulate, life-changing understanding of their identity and direction—over a few months or even a few days. But a participant's journey to clarity actually begins before they start Younique, and it continues long after they finish. That's what the Clarity Spiral describes. The Clarity Spiral master tool is not exactly a stage in the Younique process. Rather, it is a way to describe the much longer process of clarity that arches over your whole life. It is a process you repeat over and over again, and unlike a guided retreat or a course you take in school, you're usually not taking steps one at a time but at the same time. The practices of the Clarity Spiral don't march in single file but dance in a continuous weave.

So let's unpack each of the four practices—the essential, lifelong commitments—of personal clarity. We'll also explore how to take these steps while "keeping in step with the Spirit" and not running ahead of him (Gal. 5:25 NIV). But remember, without commitment to these four practices, every life planning tool under the sun—even Younique—is a waste of time.

Most of all, keep in mind that these essential practices are the continual on-ramps to your life design journey. We must never lose the sense of journey. As Os Guinness proclaims, "Journeying is the most apt metaphor for human life itself . . . the human odyssey at its highest is life with a quest for purpose, meaning, destination, and home."[5]

Part Two

THE FOUR PRACTICES

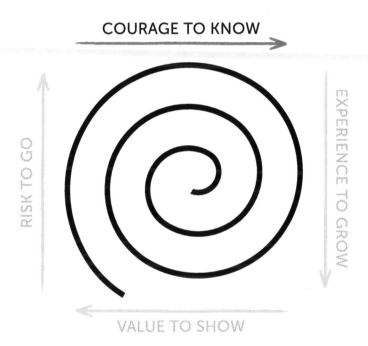

Chapter 3

COURAGE TO KNOW

*How the Worst Meeting with My Boss
Became the Best Day for My Career*

*"You can only give as much as you know about yourself to as
much as you know about God."*

–Peter Barnes

I had finally completed my second four-year degree, a master of theology in pastoral leadership. After plugging away for thirty hours a week as an engineer with a wife and two babies in tow, the grueling journey was now over. I was hungry to get started in a full-time ministry position in a church—discipling people, leading teams, and launching programs.

Actually, that's a bit of a fib. All I really wanted to do was preach. But it's common to have to "pay your dues" in church work before you earn the right to pulpit time. So I was ready to endure the grunt-work on the way to fulfilling my dream of becoming a legendary communicator.

There was no doubt I was going to be the next John Ortberg,

by the way. If you don't know that name, he was the teaching pastor at America's largest church during my seminary days— Willow Creek Community Church in Greater Chicago. He preached like a sage on stage. His eloquence flowed with casual and relatable ease and the perfect dash of humor. It was obviously just my style.

So as seminary was winding up, I looked only for pastoral positions in churches that religiously followed the Willow Creek way of "doing church." The good news was that Clear Creek Community Church in the greater Houston area fit the bill and was hiring. The bad news was that Bruce Wesley, the senior pastor, wasn't hiring a *teaching* pastor; his only opening was for a *children's* pastor, and he was fervently recruiting me for the position.

Obviously Bruce was crazy. Children's pastor? *Are you kidding me?* I had just spent half a decade learning Greek and Hebrew, the original languages of the Bible. I wasn't about to start rolling around with kids in the church nursery!

But Bruce promised to give me a little teaching time on Sunday mornings and Wednesday nights. Hmmm . . . I figured that was enough to show him the communicator I was destined to be.

So I got my foot in the door of the right church—the platform for my teaching trajectory. My ego struggled a bit with the idea of being a "children's pastor" so I negotiated my way into the official title of "Life Development Pastor." It was just vague enough that I wouldn't lose credibility with my seminary buddies. (Children's ministers who haven't given up reading yet, please forgive me.)

The best news was that Clear Creek was growing by leaps and bounds. Every month dozens of families were joining our church. Giving was up and to the right. We would be hiring a teaching pastor soon—I could see it on the horizon. I was only two years away from being Houston's very own John Ortberg.

My Worst Meeting Ever

Finally the day came for Bruce to promote me to Teaching Pastor. I couldn't wait. I was making a huge impact leading the children's area, missions ministries, and small groups. I was teaching on a regular basis to glowing reviews. So I strolled into Bruce's office and took my seat, eager for my job review.

After ten minutes of small talk Bruce dropped a bomb. "We are going to look *outside* the church to hire a teaching pastor," he revealed.

Shock. Disbelief. Betrayal.

Clearly Bruce had failed to consider God's plan for my life. While my face revealed utter disappointment, my mind was rehearsing my immediate resignation. I was ready to pack my entire life into a U-Haul and abandon Bruce and everyone else at Clear Creek Community Church.

But I didn't. Little did I know it would become the best day of my career. How so, you might wonder? In short I learned the importance of a new kind of courage.

The first essential for visionary living is to take a

> I learned the importance of a new kind of courage.

bold and courageous stance. But it's not just any kind of courage you need—it's courage to know yourself. Think of that courage as your starting block position as you sprint into the Clarity Spiral.

It's a logical place to begin, is it not? The problem is that most people are not fully aware of their greatest abilities and deepest passions. When it comes to our limitations, we prefer blind spots to brutal facts. When it comes to our strengths we position the abilities we like over the strengths we live. Ben Franklin once said there are three hard things: diamonds, steel, and knowing oneself. Physicist Richard Feynman wrote, "The first principle is that you must not fool yourself, and you are the easiest person to fool."

Bruce's declaration that I would not be the next John Ortberg was brutal. It sent me into a tailspin for weeks and even months. But it was also beautiful, because he was helping me to see who God made me to be. It still stands as the worst meeting I have ever had with a boss. But it started the adventure of a lifetime. That day Bruce told me I was a leader first and a teacher second: I was a solid-"B" communicator but an "A-plus" leader. He was correct in his evaluation, but I couldn't see it yet. I was operating out of a self-projection that needed to be confronted. But because of Bruce's "brutiful" honesty that day, the courage to know myself would begin to stir like never before.

> We prefer blind spots to brutal facts. We position the abilities we like over the strengths we live.

What about you? How well do you *really* know yourself?

My Balder and Fatter Self

We must commit to the bold idea that we don't automatically look objectively in the mirror when it comes to our abilities. At age 48, I am fully aware that I have gained a few pounds here and there. But I still look fairly good in the morning mirror . . . or so I think.

At a recent church conference a good friend posted a pic of a guy speaking. His waistline bulge was pushing the limits of his button-down. Swiping through Instagram, I was momentarily embarrassed for the dude when I saw that picture. Then I took a second glance. Big mistake: I discovered that the speaker was *me*!

I was simultaneously horrified and perplexed—I didn't see that bulge in the mirror the morning of my speaking event. Determined to solve the mystery I discovered that I have a crazy habit: I subconsciously suck in my tummy at all times in front of the mirror! When I step out of the shower or slip on my jeans, the me that I see is not the real me. My reflexes are perfectly designed to keep me fooling myself.

But it gets better. I am also growing a bald spot on my head that presently is bigger than a silver dollar and smaller than a Cracker Barrel pancake. It's the perfect size to remain completely hidden when I turn from side to side shaving in the morning. I simply don't see it until someone posts a picture of the back of my head.

In my own eyes, I'm the fit and trim 33-year-old Will Mancini every day. But the rest of the world sees my balder and fatter self.

Now, I joke with you about the "me" that I don't want to see. But believe it or not, the same principle applies with things about myself that are noble, things I might be proud of if I gave myself the chance to see them. In my temporarily devastating review with Bruce, there were strong leadership gifts—or so Bruce believed—sitting in my

> "The first principle is that you must not fool yourself, and you are the easiest person to fool."
> –Richard Feynman

blind spot, hidden behind the ministry gifting I wished I had. My False Self had me stubbornly fleeing not from something embarrassing but from something beautiful.

In the same way, I have found that even the most self-aware followers of Christ still have much to learn about their own stories, values, talents, and passions. God made each person a hidden treasure, but we are hidden most of all from ourselves. We look into the mirror every day, but we don't automatically see the essential version of ourselves. Therefore we must find a crisper, cleaner, and clearer self-portrait.

The Four Great Barriers to Self-Awareness

The great thing about self-awareness is that it is readily accessible to anyone who wants it. This chapter constitutes your invitation to attend University of You ("UU" for short), and the tuition costs nothing.

Unfortunately, many people never enroll because of four barriers that stand between us and self-awareness. In my experience almost all people deal with some if not all four of these obstacles. Let's size them up in turn.

Barrier One: The Expectation of Others

The first and most common barrier consists of the expectations other people lay on you—the Me Others Want Me to Be.

When you were still in a bassinet, did Mom dress you up like a ballerina or did Uncle Johnny give you a furry football? Almost everyone I meet has someone—a parent or coach, a brother or sister, an aunt or uncle, a teacher or neighbor, a grandparent or friend—who helped create a force-field of expectations in their lives. Layered year upon year upon year, these expectations become part of life's fabric. Our assumptions and aspirations are guided by them, and we're often not aware of it. Some of these people meant well . . . others, perhaps, not so much. Sometimes they laid expectations on us through proud smiles and loud praise, other times through mean scolding and mockery.

In the end, the whys and hows don't matter. What matters is that we were placed without our knowing consent in a room designed and furnished for us by others. It might be home. It might also be prison. But until we see it for what it is, we'll never be able to break through the invisible bars of the cage.

I routinely run into people whose entire career choices were guided by cursory comments made by a parent. My journey to becoming a chemical engineer started with just such a brief moment. In third grade I came home with all "A's" on my report card with the exception of science. I had a big fat "C" in that class, messing up my perfect record (not to mention costing me

> You are not a steward of someone else's opinion of you or dream for you, no matter how much they love you.

that free banana split at Baskin Robbins). I can remember my Dad, a brilliant engineer, getting quiet. He positioned his head to look straight into my eyes. Then he spoke with authority and intensity: "Son"—dramatic pause—*"Mancinis don't make 'C's' in science."*

Enough said. That day I didn't become a Christian, but I did pray to receive science into my life.

In my coaching work at Younique, I always ask people to reverse-engineer their job choices. Think hard: how much is your current line of work impacted by the expectations of others? Why do you do what you do? Whom are you trying to make happy, and how?

God will never hold you accountable to live up to the expectation of another person. That person will be personally accountable to God and so will you. You are not a steward of someone else's *opinion of you* or *dream for you*, no matter how much *they love you.*

Barrier Two: The Imitation of Success

If expectation doesn't get us, imitation just might—the Me That's Sexiest to See. It's funny how a flash of talent can distract your inner compass. It's as if someone else's magnet moves the needle off of your own true north. Every day we see a parade of successful people from nightly news to social media to the other guy who got the promotion at work, and we want to get the success they got the way they got it. It doesn't matter how that success is defined—it may be a cultural definition or it may be biblical one—it still becomes a barrier to your self-awareness.

Every industry has its rock stars that awaken the impulse to imitate, even the church. It's actually been going on since the Book of Acts. Take Simon of Samaria, for example, who had been a sorcerer of sorts with a pretty successful track record before he believed the gospel (Acts 8:14-24). When Simon saw Peter and John lay hands on people and perform miracles by the Spirit, he immediately offered money to buy the power and imitate the apostolic calling that wasn't his own. Peter, discerning his ungodly motives, harshly corrected him.

> Imitate the character of godly people, but don't cut and paste their charisma.

Almost two thousand years later, as a budding seminary student in the 90s, I walked by a monumental sign on campus every day that said, "Preach the Word." Every day the students took a big timeout called "chapel service," during which someone would "preach the word." The communication event was quite important at that place, so much so that my buddies and I began to imitate the style of well-known preachers. Some practiced the boom of deep-voiced pulpiteers like Chuck Swindoll. Others emulated the comic sniffle of the world-class teacher on campus, Howard Hendricks.

If I could go back in time, what would I say to my younger self? I would declare: "Imitate the character of godly people, but don't cut and paste their charisma; find your own. Learn from successful leaders, but don't photocopy their calling. You can't be anything you want to be, but you can be everything God wants you to be. If you try to fulfill someone else's calling, who will fulfill yours?" I would have jumped up and down to tell that young Will Mancini, "Stop trying to be *the next John Ortberg* and become *the first Will Mancini.*"

Kevin Kelly is the co-founder of *Wired* magazine and the co-founder of several non-profits. Listen to his words on imitation:

> The great temptation that people have is they want to be someone else, they want to be in someone else's movie. They want to be the best rock star, and there are so many of those already that you can only wind up imitating somebody in that slot. To me, success is you make your own slot. You have a new slot that didn't exist before.[6]

God didn't design you to run in someone else's slot. Find your own calling, your own voice, your own style, your unique contribution. Remember as you walk the journey to have faith in your own createdness.

Barrier Three: The Captivation of Money

Net worth is the biggest obstacle for many people. Some are allured by wealth because it's easy to believe that money buys comfort and that comfort is happiness. Others—especially those with a hot competitive streak—love money as the be-all-end-all, neat-and-tidy, black-and-white measure of success (or, in Christian circles, "blessing") and basis for comparison with others. Still other people endured anxiety, disruption, and shame by growing up poorer than the people around them, and they swear to do whatever it takes to keep from experiencing that again.

Whatever the reason, salary makes us slaves. It's the Me that Someone Pays Me to Be. When money is the ultimate goal, pursuing the clarity of personal calling falls to the wayside as a waste of time. Cash is the ultimate caller, not God. "Captivation" is an appropriate word, because a life of chasing money can create zombie-like living that keeps you stuck in a trance for long time. It can be a rut that people ride to their grave. Scripture couldn't be clearer on this subject: "For the love of money is a root of all kinds of evil, and by craving it, some have wandered away from the faith and pierced themselves with many griefs" (1 Tim. 6:10).

My ballistic arc into chemical engineering influenced by my dad's expectations got a big boost from a magazine article I read when I was preparing for college. The story ranked the top professions by entry-level salary for new college graduates. "Chemical engineer" led the field. That's all I needed to know. I had excelled at the sciences ever since my dad's lecture, and I had had a high school chemistry teacher—Mr. Krug—whom I so admired that I engaged the subject because he was so engaging. So when chemical engineering flashed a little "green" at me, I was a sucker for it.

After graduating from Penn State I won the salary I had been gunning for with a job in the oilfields of Texas. Before making the drive with my earthly belongings, I bought a used Mercedes sedan that was my pride and (supposed to be) joy. It communicated to everyone—most of all to me—that I had made it.

I pulled into the parking space at my apartment in a dusty west Texas town—a German luxury car in a lot entirely populated with American pickup trucks. The next morning, I discovered that my hood ornament had been wrenched off in the middle of the night. Fuming, I soon made an appointment with the nearest dealer to have it replaced. The next morning, *that* one was stolen. I was beside myself.

What in the world was I fighting to preserve? A piece of metal on the front of the machine that got me to work—*and* a piece of my soul, the successful self that I wanted myself and other people to see.

Jesus wasn't messing around when he admonished, "Watch out and be on guard against all greed, because one's life is not in the abundance of his possessions" (Luke 12:15). When we make our stuff into the proxy for our selves, we lose track of who we really are. For some people, that's the whole point—they're afraid or ashamed of their actual self and want to buy a replacement. I'm here to urge you not to do that. I promise you that the Called Self God implanted in you when he made you is immeasurably better than anything money can buy.

Barrier Four: The Preoccupation with Activity

All barriers to self-awareness are hidden in plain sight, and none more than the stream of activity we swim in every day. The higher and faster the river flows, the more our minds are flooded with distractions from who we really are and what we're made to do. You could call this the Me Time Makes of Me.

We have obligations to our employer, obligations to our kids, obligations to our church, and obligations to our friends that keep us moving—because if we don't do it, who will? Stacked on top—or supporting them underneath?—are our obligations to ourselves: the hobbies we're committed to pursue, the image we want to maintain, and our instinct that we're missing out if we don't pack every moment with motion.

We might think our lives are full because of how busy we are, but that's not so. Seneca pronounced, "Living is the least important activity of the preoccupied man." When our time is consumed with what we're doing, our minds are not. The more we have going on, the more we believe our activities to be absolute, as unalterable as gravity and the sun rising every morning. Activity takes on a life of its own. It is the master we dare not question, or maybe that we don't know how to question. At its most advanced stage it eludes recognition, as continuous and unnoticed as our breath. Our human being is completely obscured by our human doing. Seneca again: "This is what happens when you hurry through a maze; the faster you go, the worse you are entangled."

In bold contrast to the hurried life, God made the Sabbath for the benefit of humankind. Believe it or not, *time* is the first thing that God ever called "holy" (Gen. 2:3). The regular day of rest is sacred for several reasons, but I believe that one of them is the holy ground it fences off where you can look at what you're doing with the rest of your time. You meet God there; you hear his voice calling, as to Adam in the garden, "Where are you?" It takes sincere effort and follow-through to make enough sacred space in your activities to take the journey to clarity, but the productive energy generated by knowing your life's calling more than makes up for it.

When we've seen through our activity to see ourselves, we can live our lives, as Thoreau put it, "only earnest to secure the kernels of time" and not to "exaggerate the value of the husk." We can finally discriminate between which activities are essential to our Called Self and which are not. All of us should strive to become like John Wesley, who testified, "Though I am always in haste, I am never in a hurry."

The Ultimate Barrier: The Projection of Self

These four barriers to self-awareness—the expectation of others, the imitation of success, the captivation of money, and the preoccupation with activity—are not obstacles that we encounter one at a time. Rather, they are four blocks of different material, combined in different proportions and shapes in each of us, that together compose the single major barrier we bump into over and over again as we go through life. Ready to find out what it is? *It's you. You* are your biggest barrier to knowing you.

When I say *you*, I don't mean your true self but what I call *the projection of self*. Picture a projector in my heart that's running virtually all the time, casting its image on the surface that you see and hear when you encounter me. It isn't the real me; it's the Me I Want to Be. It shines so bright that not only does it keep you from seeing the real me, but it keeps me from seeing it too.

I used to be described well by something Parker Palmer wrote: "There is a great gulf between the way my ego wants to identify me, with its protective masks and self-serving fictions, and my true self."[7] As a young pastor I pursued counseling from a retired pastor in my church named Bill. Bill kept telling me that I wasn't okay with myself. I resisted this notion tooth and nail. I just could not see what he was talking about. "'Not okay with myself?'" I thought. "Bill, either you are completely wrong—because I feel 100% okay with myself—or else I am completely self-deceived."

After a while I grumbled to a friend how the whole counseling exercise seemed like a total waste of time, and with one sentence from him the scales fell off my eyes. "Will," he said, "you *are* 100% okay with yourself: *the self you are trying to project.*"

There it was; it was so obvious. I was okay with my affinity for the teaching pastor career in a growing church. I was okay with the image of an up-and-coming, go-getting, charismatic ministry dynamo. I was okay with being the head of an idyllic household.

Do you remember *The Wizard of Oz*? There's a brilliant moment when Dorothy and her friends return to the wizard the second time. Her dog Toto pulls away a curtain to reveal that an unimpressive, unassuming man is operating the terrifying projection of the Great and Powerful Oz. When he attracts their attention, the projection bellows, "Pay no attention to the man behind the curtain." Yet once the man behind the projection is revealed, unable to avoid exposure, it actually releases him from being what he wasn't and he flies home.

You are "the man behind the curtain." Your projection of self is trying to keep everyone, including yourself, from seeing who you are. But you too can shut the projection down and be liberated to become all God imagined you to be. You too can fly home.

The Me God Created Me to Be

What's on the other side of these great barriers to self-awareness? The break-thru to the real you. Most people's true self is a buried treasure. It stays under-realized and therefore under-appreciated and under-utilized. We simply have to do some digging. And the first quality you need to begin the excavation is the courage to do so.

Believing the gospel of Jesus Christ is crucial to gaining that courage. That's because the Me I Want to Be—the projection of self—covers up the me I actually am. As I said before, my wishful self-concept may cover up good qualities that I don't recognize (such as the leadership gifts seen by my boss, Bruce), but it also covers up qualities I don't want to own up to (such as "my balder, fatter self"). My projection of self covers up the heavy duty kinds of impurity and pride rooted deeply in my life. And it covers up the truth that I can't clean up my sinful, messy self, even with the grittiest self-improvement tools.

No one naturally wants to see the truth of their own depravity. It limits how much "courage to know" any person will exercise. A person might want to know themselves, but no one wants to know *that* about themselves. Unfortunately, we can't become the person God dreamed us to be unless we come to know who we are without him.

That's why the gospel liberates us to know ourselves fully. The gospel shows us that when we add up all of our dumb mistakes, devilish motives, and defiled moments, God's love adds up even more. It tells us that the Son of God died and rose for us so we could live a new life for him. It reveals to us that "we are [God's] workmanship, created in Christ Jesus for good works, which God prepared ahead of time for us to do" (Eph. 2:10). When you know you are completely loved and freely forgiven despite yourself, you can then begin to become yourself.

Imagine for a moment two versions of you standing side by side. The first version standing on one side is the you that you wish you were. The second version standing on the other side is the you that God dreamed you to be. Now imagine that you could actually see both versions of you, but you can only pick one to live out for the rest of your life. I have no doubt that if you could truly see both, you would pick God's dream of you every single time.

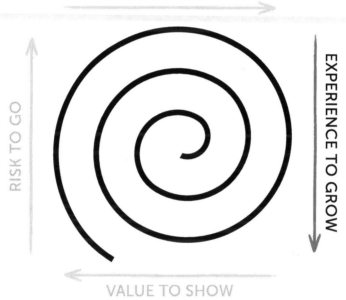

Chapter 4

EXPERIENCE TO GROW

The Fastest Way to Love Your Work, Using This Uncommon Practice That Anyone Can Master

"Many lives have a mystical sense, but not everyone reads it aright. More often than not it is given to us in cryptic form, and when we fail to decipher it, we despair because our lives seem meaningless. The secret of a great life is often a man's success in deciphering the mysterious symbols vouchsafed to him, understanding them and so learning to walk in the true path."

–Aleksandr Solzhenitsyn

The second essential practice of the Clarity Spiral is experience, but not just any experience. It's the experience which enables growth. It's experience that accelerates how you make your best contribution to the world. While "courage to know" gets you started, it's "experience to grow" that keeps it sustained. Working hand in hand, these two commitments make you an

41

unstoppable learner as you pursue your life vision.

Another way to think of it is this: once you truly have the courage to know yourself, every experience becomes a gift. Everything speaks. Or, as it's said, "When the student is ready the teacher will appear."

For example, let's say you helped your brother do his taxes. When you are done you can learn more about yourself. Did you have a knack for the task or not? What aspect did you enjoy the most—doing the math, conducting the interview, or neatly organizing the entire process?

> Once you truly have the courage to know yourself, every experience becomes a gift.

Please note that experience is the not best teacher; *evaluated* experience is. If experience taught people all by itself, people the same age would all have equal wisdom. Clearly, some people learn better from their experiences than others.

The uncommon practice that anyone can master is to refuse to let your work experiences go by unexamined. With the simple commitment of reflecting on seasons of your work past and present, each month of your life becomes a step on a ladder, taking you up, up, up to a clearer vantage point. But most people don't pay attention and they continue to march in place not allowing their experiences to elevate them.

Trial-and-Error Lifestyle

So how do you squeeze your experiences like a juicer to get every last drop of insight from them? You start by acknowledging some bad news and good news.

The bad news is simple—you can't microwave the process. You don't get break-thru in the drive-thru.[8] Finding your groove takes time. You must invite yourself into a trial-and-error lifestyle. "Experience to grow" asks us to embrace experimentation with how we use our time. Do you work better with people, things, or ideas? Evaluated experience will let you know. Do you excel at persuasion, painting, or planning? Evaluated experience will whisper the answer. Do you prefer quiet one-on-one settings or highly charged team dynamics? Do it and you will know. There is no shortcut around the time it will take to find out.

Now for the good news: the longer you have lived and worked, the more experience you have to revisit and evaluate. And even better: you can benefit from your bad experiences as much as the good ones. How so? Work tasks that you hated bring great clarity—it's clear that you weren't standing in your sweet spot while doing them. Over time, your good experiences develop your confidence and your bad experiences build your convictions—conviction about what you *don't* want to do or how you *don't* want to treat people. So don't worry about that job that grew tired or that boss that got you fired. Pay close attention and you'll find the work that keeps you wired.

Meet two recent college grads in my life: Margaret is going into PR and Adeline is a speech pathologist. Both of them chose their majors based on a career assessment and encouragement from parents. While both are very excited about their new jobs the stats say that only 27% of college grads will pursue a career related to their major.[9] So there is a one in four chance that PR and speech pathology will stick. So the question is, will they utilize their first couple of years as an "experience to grow" season? Will they jump into their careers with a willingness to learn, grow, adapt, and zero in on the next stage of their Clarity Spiral? Or will they get stuck on

> Experience is not the best teacher; evaluated experience is.

train tracks of the company's needs and parents' expectations? It's so easy to get into a rut.

In Part Two we'll share some specifics on how to mine your work history for gems of insight as you dig into your passion and ability. For now the key points to remember are these: to find your life calling, make time your friend. To design work you love, reflect on what your life experiences have been telling.

Three Big Checkpoints

To fully appreciate the long trajectory of your "experience to grow" opportunity, consider three line diagrams that represent your life (figure 1).

The first is your Life Line. It simply represents chronological time moving ahead at a constant rate. The average life expectancy today in the United States is around 80 years. This creates a tidy timeline with four 20-year quarters that introduce three significant life checkpoints.

Culture has ingrained the midlife stereotype in our minds for years. Guys used to get hair plugs, but now most of us just shave our heads. I will only confess to two things while going though my own midlife crisis: buying a 2-door sport version SUV and experimenting with "camo" in the salon to turn down my emerging grey hair.

The midlife crisis is when men and women turn forty-something and start questioning their identity and self-confidence based on several factors: marriage, career, parents, children, and the physical effects of aging. It is life's halftime and most people go through their own locker-room evaluation and pep-talk.

But in recent years the classic season of the midlife crisis has multiplied up and down about twenty years. The twenty-somethings are having what is called the "quarterlife crisis." And

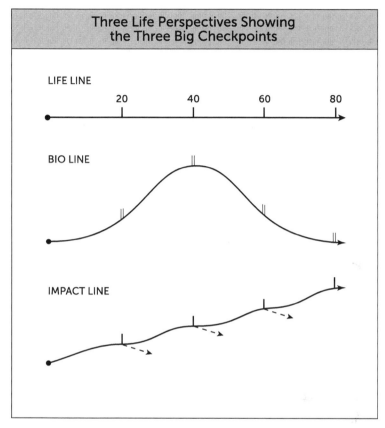

Figure 1

sixty-somethings are having—you guessed it—a "three-quarterlife" crisis. These correspond with our three big checkpoints.

The quarterlife crisis is a time of stress and soul-searching at the intersection of adolescence and entering a career. When twenty-somethings get serious about engaging the real world, there are some big questions to ask. According to some studies, 86% of Millennials experience anxiety related to job performance, finances, and career change. Damian Barr, author of the book, *Get It Together: A Guide to Surviving your Quarterlife*

Crisis, reports that the crisis usually lasts around two years and often begins with the feeling of being "locked in" to a job.[10] Janet, a frustrated 25-year-old in restaurant management, shared with me, "I'm in a slump at work and I don't know what to do about it. Despite the fact that I am performing well, I feel like I can't get my feet underneath me." The turmoil in Janet's tone was deep. The job is not completely wrong, but it's not completely right either. She feels paralyzed.

The bright side of the quarterlife crisis is that you still have most of your life in front of you. But it's not so with the three-quarterlife crisis. Men and women in their sixties face the pressure of precious little time. Tick-tock, tick-tock. How will you use the last decade or two, if the Lord wills? Move closer to the grandkids? Travel more? Shift into a more meaningful part-time occupation? It's a natural time to reconsider life's big questions again. And with most sand at the bottom of the hourglass, the soul's craving to live by a set of values as clear and solid as diamonds grows stronger than ever before.

What do we do with the knowledge that we have these three big checkpoints in life? I like to think of them as the big pitstops along life's racetrack. If the average person walks about 10,000 steps a day, you might think of this as your 73 million-step checkup every 20 years.

The Line That Keeps Rising

Let's continue by looking at the Bio Line in figure 1. This chart depicts the way that many people view their biological life-cycle. People feel the capabilities of their bodies, minds, and emotions rising to hit peak on the way to age 40 and then sliding downhill after that. Table 1 shows what the participants in one study answered when they were asked what age they thought men and women peak in different areas.[11]

As a 48-year-old, I have to admit that there is some truth to people's perceptions. I am losing muscle mass and bone density each year. New wrinkles chart their course. My late-night work hours are much less productive than they used to be. If that wasn't bad enough, doctors are beginning to demand more access to more regions of my body more often. Even with all of the best lotions, treatments, injections, or surgeries, I can no longer reverse this downward slope.

But it's not just the physical effects of aging that people associate with age 40. Many people picture age 40 as the top of the hill because they think that they are supposed to have "arrived" somewhere by that time. They expect to have peaked in accomplishment, status, or fame by then. Or they picture age 40 as the year the "success train" pulls away from the station— if you've managed to get aboard already, more success awaits, but if not, you missed your last chance.

A Closer Look at the Bio Line: Average Perceptions of Peak Age		
AREA	MEN	WOMEN
Fitness	31	33
Attractiveness	31	34
Sexual	34	34
Creative	35	37
Mental	39	42

Table 1

But is that really how life works? Thanks to God's grace, it is not. "The hill" that peaks at age 40 does have biological implications but it is not the full or final picture of your life's value. We need not despair as we lose our hair. Someday my physical body will be pushing daisies, but it's not the end of my life—only the end of my lifetime on earth.

As you stare at the Bio Line and realize that you can't do anything to stop the decay of your physical body, there is one last timeline to give us hope. What is true biologically is not true holistically. Figure 1 shows a third line called the Impact Line. I believe it is God's will for you to make an increasing impact and life contribution as you navigate these three checkpoints and as the Lord continues to give you the time.

In our current culture, it's easy to spot a bias against the elderly in many job settings. Many leaders who come through our Younique Vision Journeys testify to the perceived loss of relevance based on age. A worldly perception can erroneously equate a person's Impact Line with their Bio Line: decreasing as life crosses over the midline. But with a holistic view that takes into consideration spiritual authority, deeper relationships, growing wisdom, increased perspective, sharpened talent, and much more, we see that a person's golden years can be the most productive in their entire life.

> What is true biologically is not true holistically.

The final observation to make about the Impact Line is that a growing contribution at each big checkpoint is not automatic. Note that the dotted line at each checkpoint shows the possibility of declining influence depending on how one navigates the transition season. There is a reason that these are called crisis points. Some people don't recover. At every checkpoint or crisis point, people either break through or break down. It's your call.

The watershed difference between the two alternatives is whether you seize the opportunities to grow from your experiences. You get the opportunity each day to practice the trial-and-error lifestyle and learn along the way. And you get the opportunity at the three big checkpoints to gain insight from your journey and design your life afresh. Will you see increased life contribution through each stage of your life from your "experience to grow"?

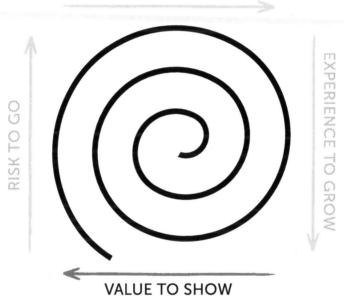

COURAGE TO KNOW

RISK TO GO

EXPERIENCE TO GROW

VALUE TO SHOW

Chapter 5

VALUE TO SHOW

One Killer Action Step to Make Any Job Better Today on the Way to Your Dream Job Tomorrow

"He makes things get. Wherever he is, he makes things move."

–Abraham Lincoln, on Ulysses S. Grant

As you get to know yourself ("courage to know") and learn from your work experiences ("experience to grow") you will soon make yourself more valuable. The third essential practice to life design is all about value, but not just any value: it's "value to show" your employer for the sake of advancing your calling.

"Value to show" means striving for the continual refinement of your role description in your current occupation or place of employment. It means that you proactively broker a great exchange—you bring more contribution *to* your work and you get more vitality *at* your work. That's aligning your 9-to-5 time with your divine design.

How I Got a 20% Raise After My Salary Capped

The fun thing is that you never stop practicing "value to show." Sixteen years into my consulting career my salary topped out. I had sold my company to a large non-profit years earlier. Due to certain stipulations in this particular non-profit my salary reached its max. Nevertheless I was able to negotiate a 20% raise. How? In short, I showed how I could continue to grow the consultancy while working four days a week, not five, for the same salary. My boss happily agreed.

Why did I make that move? Was I looking for a perpetual three-day weekend? No, I wanted to increase my value to the world by starting Younique, which includes writing this book. I was creating room for another vocational "vehicle" in my life.

The "value to show" practice introduces a way of approaching life that is frankly quite rare. Most people settle for the slots that employers provide. Most people haven't given themselves permission to negotiate with their supervisor. Work begins to feel like life on a conveyor belt. You feel intimidated by your boss. Your treadmill job continues rolling day after day after day. It's amazing to me how many people don't second-guess

> Most people settle for the slots that employers provide.

the best way to invest their talents and time on behalf of their employer. (By the way, if you are a boss, business owner, company founder, freelancer, volunteer, or stay-at-home mom or dad, don't worry; the same principles apply, as I'll illustrate later in the chapter.)

Let's start by asserting a base premise for our conversation: if you are doing the same job the same way you did last year, you are not growing. This is an unacceptable condition if you are walking the Clarity Spiral.

I do realize that some personalities are more progress- and change-oriented than others. And the world needs people who excel at routines. I am not talking about change for the sake of change. I am talking about maximizing and optimizing your one and only life where you are today. No matter who you are and no matter how you are called, you can bring more value next year than last year.

Realtors use the phrase "highest and best use." It denotes how a property can get the maximum monetary value depending on what the land and building are used for. For example, land could be used for a single-family home, apartments, or retail space.

> If you are doing the same job the same way you did last year, you are not growing.

When you show your value at work, you are moving toward the highest and best use of your time. What is the specific use of your experiences, passions, skills, and abilities that is the highest and best use for your organization?

Now I know what you are thinking: "Will, I could *never* talk to my boss like that." Or maybe you are wondering, "Will, I thought this was a Christ-centered book. What you are proposing sounds selfish." Those are great concerns and the rest of the chapter will deal with them. I will show you how "value to show" is a sound way to honor God and serve others with your life, including your boss.

Building Blocks for Showing Value

I want to give you some simple categories to apply "design thinking" to your own role description at work. They are four different kinds of value you can provide and two different approaches to provide each one for a total of eight ways to add value at work. These are not meant to be exhaustive, but they give you a great platform to begin.

The Four Kinds of Value at Work

What does any employer want from you in the end? Return on investment. Whatever your role description or job expectation, you employer is making a financial investment into you in the form of your paycheck. You, Inc. is responsible to provide your shareholder—that is, your employer—with a valuable return. You can do this in four ways: by making money, by advancing vision, by increasing capability, and by solving problems.

Making money for the company is a pretty concrete idea and is the most direct way of communicating your value. **Advancing vision**, however, is the most important way to contribute, although vision is a less obvious and less easily measured resource than money. Moreover, to connect your value as an employee to advancing vision, your organization and your boss must have a sense of clear mission, vision, and values (and unfortunately, many don't).

Increasing capability is about making your company bigger, stronger, and faster. Your boss will see this clearly when you make it happen. And finally, **creating solutions** is about finding ways to overcome the problems that arise day in and day out. When you remove a headache for your boss, he or she will take notice—trust me. The most important ones are keeping him or her up tonight. (Do you know what they are?) And creating solutions also includes preventing problems from arising in the future.

> You, Inc. is responsible to provide your shareholder—that is, your employer—with a valuable return.

Progress and Order

To give you a little more to think about, let's look at each one of these kinds of value through the lens of bringing *progress* or bringing *order* to your employer. As an organizational consultant, I've spent years building teams, advising on hiring, and designing organizational structures. Through those experiences, I've learned that progress and order are like two big buckets that everything can fit into—every task, every man-hour, every dollar spent.

Imagine an arrow darting through the air at its target. Progress is like the tip of the arrow. Order is like the feathers on the back, called fletching, that give the arrow a stable trajectory and hold the aim. Progress has to do with attaining what the company wants but doesn't have yet; it's future-oriented. Order has to do with managing what the company already has; it's present-oriented.

For example, hiring an additional salesperson goes into the "progress" bucket. Her role is to create new clients that don't yet exist. But hiring an assistant for that salesperson goes into the "order" bucket. The assistant's role is to support the salesperson that already exists and to create order in her life—from setting appointments to booking travel to filling out the expense reports.

You can apply progress and order to time as well. Spending an hour building a strategic partnership makes progress. But an hour spent revising accounting categories for the budget makes order.

We can break down our four kinds of value into more detail using the themes of progress and order. For example, there are two basic ways of making money: increasing revenue (progress) and reducing expenses (order). By applying the progress-and-order "lens" to the the four kinds of value, we arrive at a total of eight ways of adding value at work, as summarized in table 2.

Eight Ways to Add Value at Work		
The Four Kinds of Value	**Order Orientation** *Managing what presently exists*	**Progress Orientation** *Attaining what is hoped for*
Make Money	**Reduce Expense** *"Find a cheaper supplier"* *"Negotiate lower rent"*	**Increase Revenue** *"Sell more widgets"* *"Preach on generosity"*
Advance Vision	**Strengthen Culture** *"Foster healthy unity"* *"Celebrate core values"*	**Innovate Mission** *"Design a new product"* *"Reach a new people group"*
Increase Capability	**Improve Efficiency** *"Streamline how to order"* *"Check kids in faster"*	**Expand Capacity** *"Add another product line"* *"Launch a new campus"*
Create Solutions	**Solve Problems Now** *"Answer the support line"* *"Fix the copy machine"*	**Prevent Problems Tomorrow** *"Install better firewall"* *"Diversify leadership teams"*

Table 2

One Simple Step to Add New Value

Now that we have listed what your employer is looking for, let's look at how you provide it. I'm giving you a super-simple way to start thinking about this: you can *add* something to, *increase* something in, *delete* something from, or *decrease* something in your daily work role. Sounds basic, but it works, and it applies to literally every job, no matter how monotonous it may seem.

Remember that your enemy is how you have always done things. So even though you are currently bringing value (evidenced by the paycheck you are receiving), you must increase your value. The easiest and most natural place to begin is to add something to your role description. That's the one simple step that I referred to in the subtitle to this chapter. Where can you create more value? What problem does your boss have that you can solve? How can you initiate? It might be for five minutes a day or it might be for four hours a week. It might be expected, or it might not. It might grow out of new awareness of a strength or out of a need in your business or ministry. It might be something you add onto your current workload until something can be removed later.

> The easiest and most natural place to begin adding value is to add something to your role description.

After you start things new you can look at functions you might want to spend increased time on or decreased time on. You make huge advances when you can delete a task you hate to do or a role that just doesn't feel like a good fit in favor of something better aligned with your life's call.

How I Kept a Job That I Sucked At

Let me walk you through a couple of examples of how amassing "value to show" hugely helped me on my journey of personal clarity.

At age 24, I wanted to be an engineer part-time while going to graduate school. For four months I went door to door "cold calling" at different manufacturing companies close to the seminary. Finally I scored the ideal job: the resin plant manager at Jones Blair paint company in Dallas, Texas. It covered the expenses of my growing family at only 30 hours a week. Best of all, it was 100% flexible with my class schedule.

My primary role at the plant was solving problems that occurred during our daily production of the "oil base" for oil-based industrial coatings. (Exciting stuff, by the way, don't you think?) My initial schedule was working from 4:00 A.M. to noon. Our mission was to use six batch reactors to produce 10,000 gallons of maple syrup-looking paint product each day.

During that time, I struggled as a young engineer due to the seasoned proficiency of the plant operators. Week after week, I felt like I wasn't needed—my chemical engineering credentials paled in comparison to my team's decades of experience. My boss made the plant look good on paper by having a degreed engineer in the operation, but I was not really providing much value. I knew it was a matter of time before he would let me go. And returning to job-searching mode would be a huge setback!

I needed to do something to keep this perfect opportunity. The value I needed from my employer in this case was not a raise or an opportunity to use a newly discovered talent but for them to allow me to keep a steady, flexible, well-paying job while I was in seminary. After all, I was making a lot more than my buddies who were cleaning pools and waitering. So I needed "value to show" them in return.

I decided to "show value" by **adding** two things to my role description. First, I began to **prevent problems tomorrow** (that is, I *created solutions* with a *progress* orientation). I asked my boss for permission to make the plant "ISO certified." That meant documenting every bit of detail of how we made hundreds of chemical products to prepare for increased government regulations. It also gave us a competitive advantage as a smaller production company. No one wanted to do this important but non-urgent work, and it required my technical training to complete. It also made my boss look good as he displayed the new manuals in his office as a badge of honor.

Second, I noticed that very little leadership was being exercised in the waste management area of the plant. Even though it wasn't in my role description I asked permission to spend time looking for ways to **reduce expenses** (that is, I *made money* with an *order* orientation), thus **adding** a role. I started by carving out an hour every day for three months to watch our operators collect, handle, treat, burn, and ship waste. Then I found some new technology that saved the plant $70,000 a year: a high-tech gadget that called for a "dump" only when our giant, industrial-sized compactor was full rather than paying for two pick-ups a week whether it was full or not. Next, I found a new way to better solidify our latex liquid-waste "sludge" that saved us over $100,000 per year. And of course, I made sure that my boss noticed the savings each month.

The truth is, Jones Blair didn't need me to be a resin plant manager. But my boss would have been crazy to let me go. He never second-guessed my value. And I kept my ideal job for my five years of seminary.

That wasn't my first job, but it was the first time I took initiative to design a job. I used the innate freedom in my role and I asked for permission to add to my responsibilities. Now, mark the most important benefit for my journey on the Clarity Spiral. I experienced more vitality solving new problems rather than managing a process that had been "figured out." *And I noticed.* That nugget of self-knowledge that I gained in my mid-20s was pure gold, and it would pay dividends in my future at least as rich as the value of the seminary degree that I earned while working for Jones Blair. But that was only the beginning.

How I Designed My (Almost) Dream Job

As I told you in the last chapter, my first job after seminary was Life Development (i.e., Children's) Pastor at Clear Creek Community Church in Greater Houston. I jumped on board not because I was in love with the job but because I was willing to do anything to get experience in a church on a fast growth trajectory that was really reaching unchurched people. Once I landed the job, I also wanted to make more money because—news flash—entry-level church jobs don't pay much. So I **added** duties to my role description again.

As a new church plant at the time, we were meeting in a public school. Over 25 people would show up at 5:30 A.M. every Sunday to convert the school into a church for our 9:00 A.M. worship service. The first thing I noticed was that the volunteer set-up/tear-down team was serving in a very inefficient way. They would carry everything—from speakers and sound boards to craft boxes and baby-changing stations—from a huge shed behind the school that seemed like a country mile away. The team was led by our worship pastor, who had no experience in operations or logistics.

So I asked if I could help the worship pastor with the set-up/tear-down team. He was more than glad to off-load the responsibility. My goal was simple: dramatically **improve efficiency** (that is, *increase capability* with an *order* orientation).

Within weeks I overhauled the entire process of turning the school into a church. I had no budget for the needed equipment so I found some rejected plastic containers at a chemical plant for pennies on the dollar. I can remember the first Sunday that no volunteer hand-carried anything but instead wheeled massive plastic containers, increasing our efficiency fivefold. I was learning to unleash my resourcefulness and the combination of my "maximizer" and "activator" talents.

Before the end of my first year, I asked permission to start our missions ministry. I was driven to **innovate mission** (that is, to *advance vision* with a *progress* orientation) by extending the church's passion for church planting to Mexico. I enjoyed getting out of bed on workdays more than ever as I gave time to innovative ministry development in the city of Cuernavaca.

Before the end of my second year, I hired and supervised three 20-hour-per-week staff to run the children's ministry. That allowed me to **decrease** time that I spent doing KidMin directly so that I could **increase** time in other areas. I began to **expand capacity** (that is, I *increased capability* with a *progress* orientation) by designing and implementing a leadership development process.

By the end of my third year, my title had been changed to Pastor of Spiritual Formation and Leadership Development. I spent the best hours of my day raising leaders to lead groups and training them by one-on-one mentoring. My role description in that local church was tightly wrapped around my sweet spot. I remember one week, when catching up with a dozen or so of my seminary buddies, that I was almost embarrassed to share how well things were going. Most of them were stuck in unhealthy churches or ministry jobs they didn't like.

What If You Don't Report to a "Boss"?

So how do you add "value to show" when the primary person you report to is yourself? Ironically, one of the hardest times to add things to your role description is when you have a high degree of autonomy. This freedom is often accompanied with roles in executive leadership like a company founder or president. Other roles having more innate flexibility include that of a solopreneur or the noble vocation of raising children and managing a home.

On the surface you would think that *not* having a boss would make it easier to modify your role description. And technically that is true. But in reality you don't have the luxury of an actual person to help discern the question, "What would make my boss happier right now?" Instead of having a boss to "negotiate with" or "ask permission of," you have a mental model of how you currently do your job. It is sometimes harder because you are negotiating with yourself. What do you need to add to your role description that no one will notice immediately? What do you need to give yourself permission to do differently?

Answering these questions is difficult because it often

requires more imagination, self-activation, and new habit formation. But the point is, you *can* ask yourself the questions and answer them.

Lessons Learned

My vocational odyssey, which I shared with you in this chapter taught me three crucial lessons, about the importance of "value to show" for the spiraling path up the mountain of personal clarity.

Lesson #1: You Are Responsible

In those early work experiences and in every one thereafter, I was the one responsible to increase my value. My bosses were not responsible to wring every drop of potential out of me. If they were forward-thinking enough to devote some of their time, energy, and money to invest in my development, that was great, but it ultimately wasn't their obligation. It was mine.

Jesus' parable of the talents (Matt. 25:14-30) dramatically illustrates the truth that God expects a return on the gifts he has given to every person. Creative initiative is not expected of entrepreneurs or artist-types only. Creative initiative is expected of everyone. That's the assumption of the parable; the master does not instruct *how* each person should use their talent, however much or little they have. Autonomy is given and initiative is assumed. But the most important lesson is that God does not use a cute euphemism for "playing it safe"; he calls it wicked and lazy. If you are doing the same thing the same way you did last year, be careful. Playing it safe is the most dangerous thing you can do.

You are responsible to take action. Oswald Chambers offers bracing wisdom to anyone stuck in what feels like a dead-end job:

When it comes to taking the initiative against drudgery, we have to take the first step as though there were no God. There is no point in waiting for God to help us—He will not. But once we arise, immediately we find He is there. Whenever God gives us His inspiration, suddenly taking the initiative becomes a moral issue—a matter of obedience. Then we must act to be obedient and not continue to lie down doing nothing. If we will arise and shine, drudgery will be divinely transformed.[12]

Finally, you are responsible to demonstrate your "value to show" your employer. Yes, if your boss is an attentive manager he or she will recognize what you're doing, but unfortunately many aren't. And even if your boss is attentive, they may not automatically connect the dots between your initiative and the valuable outcome. It's up to you to enable them to see the value of what their subordinate is doing just as you would want to see it if you were in their shoes.

Here are a few practical tips to point out your "value to show" without boasting:

- *Document your value and communicate it.* Send a "by the way" e-mail regarding how much money you saved the company over the last six months. If you are not sure the best way to approach your boss, try asking him or her something like, "What is the most appropriate way to initiate a conversation about the additional value I've been bringing to the company over the last six months?"

- *Always be positive, especially with your non-verbals.* Smile a lot. Laugh when people laugh. Glow with a calm confidence. Don't slouch, smirk, mutter, or putter. Discontent on display will short-circuit any attempt to show value.

- *Ask for situation-specific advice from the right people.* Usually the right person is someone with more experience or authority than the boss you are approaching. Find someone who is "on your side" and wants you to flourish. Give them precise information about what you want to say and get their input on how to approach your supervisor.

- *Before you start the job, ask "how."* Ask often how you will be evaluated and how best to communicate with your boss.

- *Pray before you appeal.* Seek the Lord's help. There is always a godly way to appeal to the person in authority over you. Remember Daniel who had God's favor to "break the rules" when he made a request to his supervisor to eat a different diet (Dan. 1:8-21).

Lesson #2: Interpret Your Experience

Every time I did something well, or I *liked* what I was doing, I took notice. I started to see patterns that clarified each next vocational step. Strategically saying "yes" to new responsibilities in my sweet spot gave me increasing leverage to say "no" to responsibilities that I wasn't well-suited for. I could humbly persuade my bosses to redistribute certain duties because they saw that they would be paid back many times by how effectively I handled the things I was good at.

Ironically, it wasn't until later that I learned just how critical this lesson is—and how hard it is sometimes to reflect upon experience deeply and accurately. Did you notice how I called my job at Clear Creek "my (almost) dream job"? The truth is, it *was* my dream job for that phase of my life, as my conversation with my seminary buddies revealed. But I couldn't yet appreciate that God was preparing me to step into a different kind of vocation in coaching and consulting.

Lesson #3: Value Is a Two-Way Street

The fundamental principle of all employment is that you bring value to your employer, and in exchange your employer brings value to you. This happens in multiple, overlapping ways.

One of the greatest kinds of value that an organization delivers to you is its own health and prosperity as an environment for doing meaningful work. It was a lot easier for me to rise from Children's—I mean, Life Development—Pastor to Pastor of Spiritual Formation and Leadership Development because I was working for an organization that was growing by leaps and bounds at the time. I could not have had anywhere near the success I attained were I not part of a successful team.

There is truth to the proverb that a rising tide lifts all boats. Because the church was winning, all of us on staff were winning. But on the other hand, by the grace of God, my vigorous labors were one of many reasons that the tide rose. In other words, the value I showed my colleagues at Clear Creek helped them just as the value they and the whole church showed helped me.

At the microeconomic level, reciprocal value means that "the worker is worthy of his wages" (Luke 10:7). It means that a fair valuation of labor stands at the nexus of *both* what the buyer (your employer) demands *and* what the supplier (you) supplies. If you abandon to your employer all the responsibility for determining what wage you're worthy of, you're not playing your part in the relationship. You become like a shopkeeper who asks a customer to tell him the price of an item on the shelf. Does that make sense? Don't let one person—your boss—dictate how much your work is worth.

Finally, "value to show" is in the eye of the beholder. When you consider how you can add value at work, realize that you must add what is valuable *to your boss* and *to your organization*. In fact, just as a GPS device plots your location by communicating with three satellites, you can identify your best way to show value by triangulating the intersection of what you can do well, what your organization requires, and what makes your boss look good. Are you trying to solve your boss's problems (as *your boss* sees them, not what *you* think your boss's problems are)? And are you contributing the highest and best use of your time to your organization's mission, vision, and values? When you can answer "yes" to these questions, you're truly showing value.

Nevertheless, sometimes there are situations where providing the best value you possibly can just doesn't seem to make a difference. There might be restrictions that box you in or forces that undermine your efforts. Or maybe your boss simply won't recognize or appreciate the value you're adding. Or maybe your employer won't compensate you accordingly because they don't have the resources or the flexibility or the vision to do so. Circumstances like these often get a person to think about looking elsewhere for employment. For that step you need the fourth practice of the Clarity Spiral—*risk to go*.

COURAGE TO KNOW

RISK TO GO

EXPERIENCE TO GROW

VALUE TO SHOW

Chapter 6

RISK TO GO

How to Overcome the Greatest Barrier We All Have to Living Our Dreams

"A ship is safe in harbor, but that's not what ships are for."[13]

Doug couldn't sleep the night before his first big day on the job.

He graduated with a finance degree but had no immediate job offers. His father, who managed a high-end furniture store, made a place for him to work the showroom floor as a salesman. After a week of preparation, which included an investment in two brand-new suits, Doug was ready for his first big day.

Or so he thought. At 2:00 A.M. he couldn't control his anxiety. He sprung from his bed and meandered his way to the bedside of his sleeping father. Nervously he woke his dad to tell him that he couldn't go to work in the morning. "I just can't see myself selling furniture, Dad!" he said to his father with whispered intensity.

To Doug's surprise, his dad wasn't that disappointed. Rather, he was inquisitive. "What do you really want to do, Doug?" his father asked.

Doug stared into the darkness of the bedroom for several minutes. Then he confessed, "I think I want to *make* furniture, Dad, not *sell* it."

Doug's hunch that night would change the trajectory of his life.

Because of his father's furniture connections, Doug had an interview at noon the next day with a custom cabinetry shop. Despite having never built a thing in his life, he was hired and given a work station among a dozen experienced carpenters. His first project was a giant custom film cabinet for Exxon. At every step of hand-making the cabinet, Doug carefully watched the experts around him. He picked up the tools and rules of the trade with astounding speed. Within four months Doug was in charge of the entire shop!

> This chapter is about the essential commitment to leave . . . and how to trade your chicken feet for a lion's heart when the time comes.

Fast-forward forty years. Doug is a master carpenter who has traveled the world. He's built everything from church steeples to miniature golf courses to art-deco museums. He has designed the layout of Chicago's swankiest clubs and built dining rooms for Saudi Arabian princes. He can make wood do anything he wants it to.

But it all started with the radical step of waking up his father—a step, I might add, that he was scared to death to take.

The scarier truth is that most people never take that kind of risk and so they never reap the big payoff. This chapter is about the essential commitment to leave . . . and how to trade your chicken feet for a lion's heart when the time comes.

The fourth essential practice to walking the Clarity Spiral is about risk, but not just any risk. I call it "risk to go," because it's the risk to leave one job for another. It's the big leap into a new vocational direction or a change in vocational "vehicles." Think of your company, non-profit, freelance role, or ministry as a vehicle for your calling. For those who find their special assignment from God, the need to make a move to a new vehicle will inevitably come.

My Four "Risk to Go" Moments

That time has come for me at several critical intersections. These became "never look back" conversations. These are the days your heart races, your palms sweat, and every detail of the hours leading up to the "big conversation" are etched into your memory forever.

Moment #1: It was a summer day in the searing heat of the West Texas desert. I came in from 38 hours "on location" looking like I had showered in dust and sand. ("On location" is the nice way of saying that you lived out of a pick-up truck in the middle of nowhere while working on a drilling rig.) That day I told my boss and district manager Tom that I was leaving my lucrative career at Schlumberger to pursue ministry. Totally nervous. Insanely convinced. No regrets.

Moment #2: It was a spring day in Houston, late in the afternoon. I recounted with gratitude the high points of all I had learned from Bruce—my boss, my mentor, and the senior pastor of Clear Creek Community Church. He had let me build my perfect role description. But I told him I needed to leave and pursue my dreams in a ministry marketing company. Crazy idea. Bet-the-farm odds. No regrets.

Moment #3: It was a cold day in January, and I was reflecting on the chilly, distant relationship I had with John, the owner of the marketing company I had left Clear Creek for three years earlier. That day I told him I was being called by God to start my own consulting firm. It just didn't make sense to expand consulting services in vision, leadership development, and disciple-making culture under the banner of an advertising agency. I needed to start a "church vision" shop. Audacious faith. Potential failure. No regrets.

Moment #4: It was November in Nashville and I had 45 minutes to pitch my consulting company as a strategic acquisition for the largest Protestant resource company in the world. The real dealmaking had happened at dinner the night before. I was ready to trade my ownership and control because this holding company wanted to fund the acceleration of the work I felt called to do. Once-in-a-lifetime opportunity. Massive risk. No regrets.

> Most people miss their greatest destiny because they settle for a really, really good job and never step into a great one.

A crucial element of the art of mastering your life's calling is knowing when and when not to leave an existing job. Most people miss their greatest destiny because they settle for a really, really good job and never step into a great one. Your good job is the enemy to your great job.

The Life Funnel

Let me define what I mean by "your great job." The kind of risk I'm talking about is not a random leap. It's not even doing something new that you merely think you'd *like* to do. As a practice of the Clarity Spiral, "risk to go" is a strict discipline.

Late in my seminary years I won the sublime privilege of spending three hours or more every week with the Yoda of Christian education, Professor Howard Hendricks. If it wasn't for that season with one of my all-time heroes, I wouldn't be writing this book. Why? Because "Prof"'s most important insight about life led me to discover the Clarity Spiral in my own life.

The insight came in the form of a whiteboard drawing. He had no name for it, but I came to call it "The Life Funnel" (figure 2). The top of your life's funnel is crowded with all of the things you *can do* for God. The bottom of your life's funnel is the One Thing you *must do* for God.

The problem with success is that it multiplies the X's at the top of your life's funnel. The more success you achieve, the more people you meet, resources you gain, and skills you learn, the more opportunities will line the top of your life's funnel. It's like

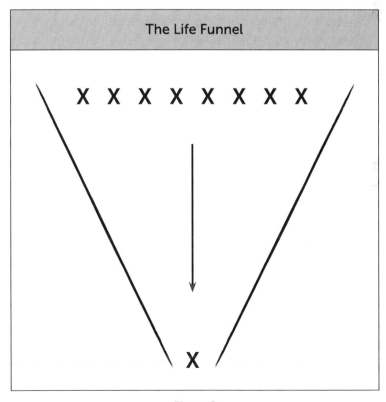

Figure 2

paper clips to a magnet. The problem is that, as more "can-dos" fill the top of the funnel, it makes it harder to see and focus in on the one thing you must do for God. The truth is that most opportunities are distractions in disguise, distractions from the "must do" that God has been preparing you for your entire life. In summarizing the funnel drawing, Prof would pronounce with haunting precision, "My greatest fear for you is not failure with your life work but success at the wrong thing."

> Most opportunities are distractions in disguise.

The key to life is not being distracted from your one "must-do" no matter how many "can-dos" come along.

When Billy Graham started a preaching tour of New England in 1950, a cynical reporter badgered him about how much money he would make from his meetings in Boston. Graham answered that he wouldn't take a dime since his salary as president of Northwestern Schools, a Christian higher-educational institution in Minnesota, was adequate for his needs. The reporter kept hounding him, certain that Graham was preaching to get rich. Graham finally reached into his pocket and handed the man a crumpled telegram he had received moments before, remarking, "Sir, if I were interested in making money, I would take advantage of something like this." It was an offer of $250,000—2.6 million of today's dollars—from a Hollywood studio to star in two films![14] This episode not only reveals how Billy Graham resisted the "captivation of money" but also how he refused to get distracted from his one "must-do" to preach the gospel to those who didn't believe it yet.

To clarify, I am not suggesting that there is only one project or job or occupation or even career that you're supposed to stick with your whole life. But I do maintain that God designed you to do One Thing in all sorts of "vehicles" that you operate through over time. Billy Graham's career is a case in point. In addition to his preaching tours, he co-founded the Lausanne Movement for World Evangelization, served as a spiritual advisor to U.S. presidents, and did much more, all because he focused on his singular calling.

Remaining rigorously fixed on your one "must-do" is actually what launches the best leaps in your career. The absoluteness of your One Thing enables you to see how relative your life is right now. When you know the One Thing about your calling that never changes, you awaken to how changeable everything else is. You take the "risk to go" because doing your One Thing more often, more purely, and more effectively matters more than whatever you're doing now.

Your career path becomes one of progressive refinement. What might appear to others as an eccentric zig-zag is actually the most direct path of a completely unique journey. What might sound like a strange, eclectic playlist to some is actually the contrasting movements of an awesome symphony with the profound sound of your Life Younique.

The One Thing That Keeps People from Their One Thing

The richness of a life's calling, fully expressed, is available to everyone. So why do so few take it? What keeps people where they are, stuck on an X at the top of their Life Funnel, while a job that fits their One Thing lies at the bottom?

Over the last twenty years I've sat across a table from hundreds of people who flash a sparkle in their eye when they talk about a "must-do" that is waiting to be named and pursued. But that suppressed flame is barely flickering, almost smothered by one word: fear.

It's not just any fear—the fear I'm talking about usually has a specific shape. It is the fear of *what might happen if I walk away from something good.* Maybe it is a job that I do very well. Maybe it is a place where I am greatly loved. Maybe it is a cushy retirement if I finish my career with the same organization. Maybe it is my mortgage payment or my neighborhood or my standard of living. Maybe it is the comfort—I might call it "health"—of my children or my spouse. Maybe it is the silent support my selfhood gets from a job title or occupational field.

The fear of what might happen if you expose any of these things to risk can be extreme. But you will never find God's greater good if you settle for your lesser good. I agree emphatically with Robert Brault: "We miss our goal not because of obstacles but because of a clear path to a lesser goal." For so many people, the biggest barrier to clarity is that thing—that lesser goal—that they are gripping with white knuckles. It's that thing they already possess. When God's better calling comes along they can't reach out and grab it.

> How will you exchange your Linus's blanket for the magic carpet ride of calling?

There's a fable about a group of sailors who were exploring an uninhabited island. Unfortunately for them, a clever monkey kept stealing their food no matter what they did to protect their supply. Finally, the sailors put a piece of fruit in a heavy glass jar whose mouth was just wide enough for the monkey to slide its hand in. When the monkey reached in and grasped the fruit it could not withdraw its fist because its grip on the fruit made its hand too large. The wriggling monkey remained helpless at the jar before the returning sailors, trapped by nothing but its unwillingness to let go.

Are you caught in the same trap? How will you exchange your Linus's blanket for the magic carpet ride of calling? Let's pry those five fingers off one at a time with five challenges that promise assurance on the other side.

Five Must-Dos to Reach Your One "Must-Do"

Must-Do #1: You Must Know God Is Calling You

I don't recommend that anyone take a risk while leaning on their own understanding and being wise in their own eyes (Prov. 3:5, 7). The kind of risk I am talking about is built on "courage to *know*" *God's will*.

This book is not about the fundamental practices of your walk with God, which includes how you learn to hear his voice. Nevertheless, employing these practices is essential. If and only if you know that God is telling you to take a risk is it wise to proceed. In fact, if God tells you to what you're here for, the risky thing is *not* to obey him.

In this respect, the Younique Life Journey is a guide for your way. As I wrote earlier, most people get clarity about God's purpose for them not by a splashy vision but by learning to discern his still, small voice on the matter. Younique is a process to do just that.

Must-Do #2: You Must See Risk as an Act of Worship

Worship is "worth-ship"—it is ascribing value to something beyond the norm. When you take the "risk to go" for God's sake, you are telling him that you're willing to give up everything—money, praise, comfort, even family—in preference to him, because he's worth it.

Paul taught that offering your body as a living sacrifice is your spiritual way of worship (Rom. 12:1). You only have one life, and it isn't yours. You are merely the steward of it. God gave it to you to give it back to him.

Must-Do #3: You Must Give the Burden of Risk Back to God

The parable of the talents, which I talked about in the last chapter, might be one of the most-often preached of Jesus' parables. Unfortunately, the familiarity defuses the shock factor. The two servants in the story who were praised by their master doubled their money. What kinds of risks were these guys taking to get returns on investment that large?

Here's a hypothetical: what if one of them said to the master, "I made a big bet on a trading expedition, and all the ships were lost at sea. I got nothin'." Do you think the master would have upbraided him? I think not, because what ticks him off is the third servant who keeps his money safe but makes no effort.

Like the master in the story, God has distributed his money to all his servants. He has a diversified portfolio; to him, it's not the end of the world if you fail, because he has plenty more out there. And he isn't merciless to those who take risks for him and make mistakes. He has abundant wealth to pick you back up, supply your needs, and get you going again. If he calls you to do a crazy thing with his resources—all that he's made you to be and have and do—let him bear the burden of the risk you take. Put the monkey on his back; he can handle it. Don't carry it on your own back.

Must-Do #4: You Must Cut Fear Down to Size

Once planted, the oak-like roots of fear grow deep and wide, entangling our motions and emotions. The towering trunks that arise become a prison. If you search for the door the silent chains of dubious logic lock it down to keep us totally trapped. Empowering fear's ecosystem is the dreaded Worst-Case Scenario. It might go something like this:

- If I quit my job to do my side-business full-time . . .

- . . . then I'll only make a quarter of my salary the first year.

- Then we won't cover our bills.

- Then we'll be evicted from our home.

- Then we'll be homeless.

- Then my spouse will leave me.

- Then I'll be all alone.

- Then I'll be a total loser.

This sort of thing lurks in our subconscious all the time but rarely comes out into the light. But does it sound 100% rational to you? Aren't there some pretty enormous assumptions, gaping omissions, and gigantic leaps? How do you know what you're going to earn the first year? Have you thoroughly measured your assets—not only what you now have but what you can get? Do you have any expense-reduction alternatives? Does no one love you enough to take you in if you were to have no place to stay? Is your spouse only in your marriage for the money? What exactly is a "loser," anyway, and how does taking a risk and coming up short make you one?

One huge practical action step: put your wordless dread in writing. It not only makes it more manageable, it cuts fear down to size and clears a way through a jungle of jitters. Once you declaw the fear critter, it might even look ridiculous—nothing *really* as scary as one would think. Tim Ferris refers to this as "fear-setting." Here is his advice:

> Define your nightmare, the absolute worst that could happen if you did what you are considering. What doubt, fears, and "what-ifs" pop up as you consider the big changes you can—or need to— make? Envision them in painstaking detail.

Would it be the end of your life? What would be the permanent impact, if any, on a scale of 1 to 10? Are these things really permanent? How likely do you think it is that they would actually happen?[15]

Must-Do #5: You Must Fear Regret More than Failure

Mark Twain sagely quipped, "Twenty years from now you will more than likely not regret the things you did but the things you didn't do."

In the end, the goal is not to dismiss fear altogether, but to make it work for you. Try it and fail? It might happen. Don't try it at all? What then? Are you prepared to live life with the aching echo of "What if?" Are you prepared to hush the gentle whisper of the Spirit and settle for the expected?

> Are you prepared to live life with the aching echo of "What if?"

At each of my "risk to go" moments, I didn't fight fear down to "0" on a scale of 1 to 10. It was still a solid "5" or "6." But I cultivated a deeper angst. The fear of missing my "must do" for God was greater still. My passion for purpose increased the fright of regret to an even higher "8" or "9." I can rehearse again that deep-seated soul confidence that says, "I would rather take the risk and fail than fail to take the risk!"

- Where would I be today if I didn't resign as an oilfield engineer?

- What would I be doing right now if I didn't explore my hunch to consult?

- What would I have missed out on if I didn't quit a great job to start something from scratch?

I am so grateful I never have to ponder these questions. What about you?

In the early 20th century, William Borden left family fortune and lucrative career potential to pursue a missionary call to China. At three critical junctures on his own "risk to go" decision-making he penned an additional two words in the margin of his Bible. At the end of high school he took a trip around the world that generated a budding passion to help the world's needy. He expressed his call to missions and wrote the phrase "No reserves," knowing he was abandoning the "expectations of others" and the "captivation of money." Years later, he graduated from Yale and took further steps toward a bold calling. He wrote the additional words, "No retreats." Sadly, on his way to the work with the Muslim Kansu people of China, he stopped in Egypt to study Arabic and died within a month. He had contracted spinal meningitis at age 25. Short in years but chock-full of yearning, Borden's life would inspire literally tens of thousands who knew of his

> I would rather take the risk and fail than fail to take the risk!

sacrifice. Days before his death he reportedly wrote two more words in the margin of his Bible: "No regrets." That's the tagline of life committed to God-honoring risk: "No reserves. No retreats. No regrets."

Through the Wardrobe

As I look back on each of my big "risk to go" moments, I shiver with delight. The memory is one of euphoria—stepping off the cliff to walk on the wind. In my case—and this is by no means true of all people who "risk to go"—at each point I was leaving a proven record of success when I stepped into the unknown. I had thought I was already flying, but until I took the risk I never knew what flight was. I had thought I was sailing, but the fullness of the wind never swelled my sails like that before.

The "can-dos" at the top of your Life Funnel are the big house you live in. You might not spend time in every room, but you've seen them, and they're familiar; you know they're there. But taking the "risk to go" is, as with Lucy Pevensie of *The Lion, the Witch, and the Wardrobe,* to enter the wardrobe into a fantastic new world.

Your must-do is behind the wardrobe door. Your housemates may not believe you, and they may not understand—not at first. But a glorious reality awaits you on the other side.

Part Three

CALLING WITHOUT FALLING

Chapter 7

DANGER

A Big Warning Sign on the Journey of Life Design

"Ability may take you to the top, but it takes character to keep you there."

–Stevie Wonder

Now that you've learned the fundamentals of the Clarity Spiral—especially after the last two chapters on "value to show" and "risk to go"—I hope you're chomping at the bit to design your life. So it probably comes as a surprise that in this chapter I'm going to pull back hard on the reins for a moment.

I am not inviting you to mere life design. I am inviting you to *gospel-centered* life design. That's why this is an especially sensitive juncture in our journey together, because a person stubbornly rebelling against God or neglecting him can get away with going their own way—for a while. The result, however, is a climb up a very different mountain than the one God has prepared for those who love him.

Even Jesus-followers, who have come to new life by the Holy Spirit, are liable to be tempted to strive for clarity in a fleshly, self-centered way. While personal fulfillment is a real outcome of life design, it is never to be the primary motivation of a believer. "Seek first the kingdom of God and His righteousness," Jesus said, "and all these things will be provided for you," including personal fulfillment in one's special calling (Matt. 6:33).

The main point isn't our fulfillment. The main point is God's glory. The subsidiary point is the benefit of the world around us. The point for *us* is to find our satisfaction when God's glory and the world's welfare are amplified through us. In short, the point is love—love of God and love of neighbor. That is the law of life design as God designed it.

This is why the gospel is crucial to life design. "We love because [God] first loved us" (1 John 4:19). Loads of people of all faiths and no faith have real love for others. But none of us can love as Jesus loved until we accept that Jesus is God's love for us. "Love consists in this: not that we loved God, but that he loved us and sent his Son to be the atoning sacrifice for our sins" (v. 10).

> **Love is the law of life design as God designed it.**

So the climb up the mountain is a climb not only to a superior level of clarity. It is also a climb to superior breadth, depth, comprehensiveness, intensity, and effectiveness of love—nothing less than an imitation of the love of Christ for us. This is what God is up to. Therefore, we can never let our work of stewarding our calling eclipse God's work in forming our character.

That character formation inevitably involves difficult situations, unwanted pain, and challenging people from time to time. That bad boss, stubborn coworker, wearisome assignment, or ugly office might be genuinely repugnant to God's ideal, but then again, you aren't yet up to God's ideal either. Those unpleasant things might be a chisel in his hand to sculpt you into his image.

Perhaps the severest curse God could lay on anyone is to give you an assignment for which your character is not yet prepared—to give you perfect clarity as to your purpose in life and the perfect opportunity to live it out only for you to succumb to the temptations that inevitably assail you when you take it on.

> We can never let our work of stewarding our calling eclipse God's work in forming our character.

(Is it fair to say that that was Adam's situation in Eden . . . ?) We should pray that God would be so merciful as not to allow us to climb further up the mountain until he has conditioned us for the rigors of the higher elevation.

So when you want to negotiate an adjustment to your job description or when you're looking for a new job opportunity, you have to examine what is driving you and what the outcome will be. Would a new vocational role be a step into greater fruitfulness or a step away from essential pruning?

A Five-Point Checklist for Your Vocational Change

God uses work—especially unpleasant work—to teach us *spiritual contentment, submission, servanthood, sacrifice,* and *suffering well*. These five marks of godly character make for a useful diagnostic tool against which to check your motives for taking your next step at work.

Here's a warning before the warning: there are two equal and opposite temptations that people fall into when they perform self-examination. One is to do it glibly or not to do it at all; these people let themselves off the hook easily. If this is your tendency, then as you consider the five marks below, if you think that one *might* address a problem in your motives, assume that it does.

But there is a ditch on the other side of the road composed of severe self-criticism and paralysis by analysis. If that's your tendency, let me gently encourage you to ask the Holy Spirit to illumine your self-understanding, then trust him to communicate clearly what you need to know. If you vaguely fear that one of the following marks *might* address a problem in your heart but you can't point to anything in particular, assume that it's your overactive conscience talking, ignore it, and move on.

Mark #1: Spiritual Contentment

Work is a useful tool in God's hand to teach *spiritual contentment*. Paul wrote stern words about people in professional ministry who were eager to wring money out of it. He alleged that they "are depraved in mind and deprived of the truth, imagining that godliness [better translated 'religion'] is a means of gain." Nevertheless, Paul says, viewed from a different angle, religious work is indeed a means of gain if it's accompanied by contentment. In fact, it's a stake in the "future . . . that which is truly life" (1 Tim. 6:5-6, 19 ESV).

This principle doesn't just pertain to ministry but to all kinds of work. Godly contentment comes from ascertaining spiritual realities so great that contentment is a genuine experience despite the worst of physical circumstances. Have you ever met a cancer patient who was full of life? Or a prisoner of war who kept their countenance?

You don't want to negotiate your role description or look for a new job from **ungodly discontent.** By contrast, Paul taught that "love does not envy" (1 Cor. 13:4). Love isn't consistent with looking at what others have, wanting it, and grumbling that you deserve it—or even more. So as you consider your next move, are you *free of covetousness*?

Mark #2: Submission

Work is a useful tool in God's hand to teach *submission*. Your employer is an authority in your life, and a follower of Jesus is commanded to respect all earthly authorities and yield to their will.

Jesus himself set the pattern. Despite being the true King, the one God had entrusted with all authority in heaven and on earth, he paid taxes (Matt. 17:24-27). Despite teaching with authority and excoriating the religious teachers of his day as "blind guides" and "hypocrites," he commanded his hearers to do what those teachers said because they were "seated in the chair of Moses" (Matt. 23:1-3, 15-19).

The Apostle Peter mandated, "Submit to every human authority because of the Lord," and he explicitly included both a brutal, egomaniacal, Christian-hating emperor (Nero) and cruel slaveowners (1 Pet. 2:13-18).

If Jesus and his apostles instructed his followers to submit to people like that, then you can submit to your boss and your organization, provided doing so doesn't constitute disobedience to God, the higher authority. Submission makes you more like Jesus himself, and in fact, he honors your submission to earthly authorities for his sake as submission to himself (Col. 3:22-24).

*You don't want to negotiate your role description or look for a new job with a **rebellious spirit**.* By contrast, Paul taught that love "is not boastful, is not arrogant, is not rude," and "is not irritable" (1 Cor. 13:4-5). Love isn't consistent with undermining authority, seizing power, or having a cocky, I-know-better attitude. So as you consider your next move, are you *humble*?

Mark #3: Servanthood

Work is a useful tool in God's hand to teach *servanthood*. How do you know if you are struggling with this? It's simple: how do you respond when someone treats you like a servant?

Three of my children found their first paid job in food service, including Abe's Cajun Kitchen and Torchy's Tacos. I think some of the most interesting professionals to watch are restaurant servers.(Yes, I consider servers professionals. What they do takes developed talent and skill, and I couldn't do it as well as they can.) Servers' whole purpose at work is to serve; *serve* is in the job title itself.

Every day servers serve people who appreciate them. They also serve people who ignore them, who make harsh demands of them, and every once in a while who even make unwanted advances on them. Every person they serve considers themselves entitled to their service. Yet regardless of a customer's character, a server is devoted to serve them.

> How do you respond when someone treats you like a servant?

When you watch a good server, you see a model of servanthood. What if we all learned to embody the same virtue in our place of work, no matter what the role? That's what Jesus did and taught: "Whoever wants to become great among you will be your servant, and whoever wants to be first among you will be a slave to all. For even the Son of Man did not come to be served, but to serve, and to give His life as a ransom for many" (Mark 10:43-45).

You don't want to negotiate your role description or look for a new job out of selfish gain. By contrast, Paul taught that love "is not self-seeking" (1 Cor. 13:5). Love isn't consistent with looking out for Number One or with making your happiness the primary concern in your vocational decisions. So as you consider your next move, are you *concerned about others*?

Mark #4: Sacrifice

Work is a useful tool in God's hand to teach *sacrifice*. In other words, your work costs you something—you're required to give of yourself for the greater good.

When you add something to your role description to show value, you ought to be investing something valuable to you—your time and energy—for the benefit of others. Likewise, when you seek to move on to a new assignment, even if you're "trading up," it shouldn't be all benefit and no cost.

If you're trying to get out of what you're doing now because it takes a toll—well, work is supposed to take a toll. Without a doubt, work can sometimes be an insatiable devourer of our time and energy—a terrible false god that demands unlimited human sacrifice. We certainly don't want to participate in idolatry (ours or our boss's). But if our service at work is actually service to the Lord, if it is actually an expression of our "living sacrifice" to him (Rom. 12:1), it had better cost us *something*. Let's have the attitude of David, who said, "I will not . . . offer burnt offerings that cost me nothing" (1 Chr. 21:24).

*You don't want to negotiate your role description or look for a new job out of **stingy self-protection**.* By contrast, Paul taught that "love is patient" and "kind"—it invests extended, costly time to help others. Love isn't consistent with a shrewd calculation to get the most while giving the least. So as you consider your next move, are you being **generous**?

Mark #5: Suffering Well

Work may be a useful tool in God's hand to teach *suffering well*. For centuries believers have endured harsh treatment from reckless bosses, supervisor-abusers, company tyrants, sexual power-players, harsh masters, and insecure authorities. If—or *when?*—you are a victim, it is not outside the plan of God for your life.

Joseph is a shining example. He was betrayed by his brothers and endured imprisonment on his vocational Clarity Spiral. But in Genesis 50:20 the facade of an earthly fate is rolled back to show heaven's truer design: "You planned evil against me; God planned it for good to bring about the present result—the survival of many people."

Yet at the end of the day, a biblical life planning process has to account for the ideal human being—Jesus himself. His special assignment on earth included the greatest degree of suffering one can know, and in the thick of it he conducted a "value to show" negotiation. In the garden of Gethsemane he inquired of his boss (God the Father) about the possibility of an alternative career path ("take this cup from me"), but he concluded with perfect submission ("nevertheless, not my will, but yours, be done," Luke 22:42). Then, "when he suffered, he did not threaten but entrusted himself to the one who judges justly" (1 Pet. 2:23). That's what it looks like to suffer well.

Your life calling does not preclude the hand of God from allowing you to suffer. In fact, suffering unjustly is part and parcel of your calling: "for you were called to this, because Christ also suffered for you, leaving you an example, that you should follow in his steps" (1 Pet. 2:20-21; see also Rom. 5:3-5; Heb. 12:5-12; Jas. 1:2-3). We don't plan for suffering, but our plan must take God's sovereign purposes into account.

Nevertheless, *you don't want to negotiate your role description or look for a new job out of **unwillingness to suffer***. Paul taught that love "bears all things, believes all things, hopes all things, endures all things" (1 Cor. 13:7). Love isn't consistent with giving up when things get hard or caring more to avoid present suffering than to gain future glory. So as you consider your next move, are you ***persevering***?

Go Slow, Go Far

Reading this chapter might make you feel like I've slammed on the brakes and brought your journey into your life's call to a screeching halt before it begins. But my intention is just the opposite.

I encourage you to start and *never stop* discovering your personal calling. I co-invented Younique lead people to break-thru, a sudden leap of clarity. But that's one portion of a lifelong journey, and there are no shortcuts.

Some people yearn for clarity because they hope to shorten the steps and get to the pinnacle of vocational fulfillment faster, but that's not how it works. God cooks with a slow-cooker, not a microwave. When we learn what God has been creating in us, that new awareness is our invitation to assist him by adding ingredients to the meal. But our conscious cooperation with God makes the final dish *taste better*; it doesn't make it *cook faster*. (For heaven's sake, "love is patient." How are you supposed to develop patience *fast*? Not even God can do that.)

I remain convinced that when you are living out the lessons of spiritual contentment, submission, servanthood, sacrifice, and suffering well, you aren't constrained in your calling; you become even freer in it. Calling isn't opposed to these virtues; it is defined by them. When they are embedded deep down in your life, they aren't a brake to the fulfillment of living your life's call; they are jet fuel.

Let me be clear: I'm the last guy to preach that suffering for the sake of suffering or self-denial for the sake of self-denial is a good thing. I'm not here to encourage some kind of heroic workplace martyrdom. I don't think God is pleased with gloomy, cynical Christians resigning themselves to wringing their bread from the sweat of their brow under callous taskmasters. Instead, I think he wants us to seek him for a taste of Eden, even if it's partial and imperfect until Jesus returns.

So there's nothing inherently wrong with hoping that a role adjustment or a new job will bring you more joy or will release you from a bad situation. All I'm saying is, those aren't big enough reasons to go for it. In the end, your "value to show" and your "risk to go" mustn't be for the sake of your pain or pleasure. They need to be for the sake of love—how you can best love God and love your neighbors. When love is your motive, you'll know what to show and when to go.

Chapter 8

CALL

The Second Greatest Decision You Will Ever Make

"Be yourself; everyone else is already taken."

–Oscar Wilde

The single most important decision in your life is whether you believe that God is who he reveals he is. The second greatest decision is whether *you* will do what God made you to do.

The portal to your potential is the belief that you were created do something that only you can do. It's a remarkable idea to ponder: God has a special assignment for you to accomplish on earth. This truth is most clearly evidenced by Ephesians 2:10: "For we are [God's] workmanship, created in Christ Jesus for good works, which God prepared ahead of time for us to do." This key verse of Scripture is rocket fuel for the journey of personal calling.

Imagine how crazy-good this truth makes your life! You are a one-of-kind design made by the most brilliant mind in the universe—God himself. Every day is an on-ramp to opportunities that put your design into action—with all of your personality, passion, gifts, and gumption. In any hour of your day, a door may open for a simple act that was prepared from before time began: speaking, deciding, touching, or building. In any moment of your week, God may orchestrate a conversation or a collision. He may prompt a prayer or a dare. He might ignite a moment that turns a frown around or a movement that turns a nation upside down.

Every day God draws the curtain and you're on center stage of this thing called your life. God dreamed you up and gets excited about how he wants to use you. He prepared good works for you to do, like a mom whipping from scratch that favorite meal.

But Ephesians doesn't say that you *will* walk in them. You are not an automaton or a stringed-up puppet. No, it says that you *should* walk in them. They are to be discerned and discovered, engaged and enjoyed. I like to say, "It's your call." It's your call*ing* because you were engineered with meticulous intent. But it's also *your call*, because it's not a given that you will experience your intent; you must choose it.

If this page were a mirror let me tell you what I see: you are a gold medalist at something. And by the way, the world is watching, waiting, even needing you to enter the games. Whatever that something is, I believe it is knowable and nameable. That's what makes Younique truly unique. The process steps in The Younique Journey take you from a general sense that there is *some*thing for you to do to declaring your *One* Thing—the one thing that changes everything. That's your Life Younique.

God-Confidence

Since I claimed that you are a divine design, allow me to

clarify that my confidence is not first in you, but in God. I find that a person's own greatness is somewhat hard to believe in their own mind, and you may be struggling with my optimism about your talent. But consider: your Creator has put within you capabilities that he hand-made and skillfully forged. He is no typical artisan; he twirls a galaxy on his finger like a fidget spinner. His code for all living things—DNA—makes Apple's latest OS look like first-grader fridge art. If you put Einstein and Shakespeare and da Vinci along with the next three geniuses you admire into one person, God is still infinitely more talented. You were made by a loving God with unfathomable resources and inexhaustible creativity.

You might consider him a master playwright too—with infinite genius, of course. He orchestrated the stage, the scenery, and the story of your life. No situation, no surprise, no sadness in your life is outside of his design and, yes, even his embrace. The stroke of his careful pen is writing an ideal story for you—a personal storybook experience that is grace-lined and gift-laden, guided by the goodness of God that is better than you can imagine.

Living the Book before Writing the Book

Although I'm writing this for you, I want you to know how my life has been impacted by these principles. I gave you some backstory earlier, but here is a little more.

Through mentoring experiences in my early twenties I believed that God had a special assignment for me. Through many ups and downs and with much trial and error, I now get to experience the thrill of my life's calling expressed in my work time every day.

I pursued three totally different careers on the journey to finding my One Thing; for seven years it was engineering, for four years it was pastoring, and for three years it was advertising. Most friends advised me not to change careers. But the conviction to do so was very strong inside of me each time, despite the risk. Without making those career shifts I would not have found my One Thing that changed everything.

From age 21 to age 34 I lived paycheck to paycheck, doing the typical stuff like getting married and having kids. During this chapter of my life I always worked for someone else. I worked for all sizes of companies ranging from Fortune 500 to midsize businesses ($200 million in revenue) to small businesses ($1-4 million in revenue) to mom-and-pop shops to churches.

I learned valuable lessons from every experience. I soaked up every book, event, and mentor that had anything to do with personal clarity and vision. I excelled at learning and problem solving. I had grown up as a quiet kid with low self-confidence, but by the end of this period, people started describing me as visionary and tenacious.

At age 35 I experienced a convergence. My three prior work disciplines—engineering, ministry and advertising—came together and found expression in a consulting ministry that I started for churches. That ministry is called Auxano, and launching it began a new chapter of living out my special assignment on earth in an accelerated way.

Through Auxano I created tools and facilitated processes where any church leadership team could experience what I call "break-thru clarity." Before long I was writing, tool-making, speaking, and training others to use my process. It was so successful that churches of all faith tribes and all sizes use the process. Most church planting networks and seminaries use our tools. Today there are ten full-time consultants and hundreds of certified leaders using our Vision Framing Process. Auxano's vision is that, by 2020, 40,000 church teams in North America would be using our process and showing others how to use it.

As special as Auxano is to me, it is only one expression of my One Thing. Five years ago I started Life Younique to bring the same kind of break-thru to individuals.

This Top Ten panel is a quick glance at some of the critical steps that marked my journey of finding and aligning my special assignment. Think of these as some of my "calls" along the way, but remember, "it's *your* call." Living from your Called Self is not automatic, so I share these with you so you can reflect on your "calls" more thoughtfully.

Ten "It's Your Call" Warm-Up Questions

1) I abandoned a great income early in my career at age 24. *What about you? You can't your find special assignment from God by chasing money. What role does money play in your current life design?*

2) I negotiated unique role descriptions with every supervisor I ever had. *What about you? No one else is responsible for your life calling. When is the last time you advocated for it with your boss?*

3) I volunteered and took ridiculous initiative to get access to people and experiences. *What about you? You will probably have to experiment and sacrifice to discover your One Thing. When was the last time you tried something new?*

4) I took a job to learn from an organization's culture even though I didn't care for the role. *What about you? You might have to advance your call by selecting a job context more than the job itself. Have you ever done that?*

5) One boss overlooked me for a position I thought I wanted and I hated life for the next eighteen months. *What about you? How will you turn negative work experiences into a highly valuable learning for finding your One Thing?*

6) After starting a business for the purpose of making money—not calling—I eventually shut it down. *What about you? You might find, like me, that money is a constant distraction from living your life calling. Have you thought about how much money you really need to be fulfilled?*

7) I abandoned my career path and established reputation in one industry to do work that I had no formal training to do. *What about you? You must trust that God has designed and prepared you for a special assignment, whether you have been formally trained or not. Have you ever made a big jump from one career to another? Are you sensing you might need to?*

8) I started a company at age 35 because I couldn't find an organization that fit my personal calling. *What about you? You may discover that starting something is the best way to express your special assignment from God. Have you started something before? Are you thinking about it again?*

9) I tripled my salary in ten months after starting a company, and even though money wasn't my motive, I made my first million before age 40. *What about you? By focusing on your calling more than focusing on money, you might be surprised how your passion and mastery translate into financial gain. Have you experienced financial gain as the natural byproduct of a focused life calling?*

10) I authored or co-authored six books and created four leadership products after I discovered my One Thing. *What about you? By focusing on your One Thing you will find that your influence expands. How has God expanded your influence lately?*

Ready to Climb?

The climb up the mountain of personal clarity isn't easy. Sometimes rain pelts down, darkness falls, or the air becomes thin. Sometimes people lose their way or can't find the path upward. It's difficult and even impossible to go it alone, much less without the right equipment for the journey.

I co-created Younique to support people with trustworthy and knowledgeable guides who can teach them the best techniques for climbing and share wisdom from their own journeys. I also built Younique to outfit climbers with all the gear they need for the trek: the five master tools.

In this book I've shared with you one master tool to discover and live your personal calling. The **Clarity Spiral** describes what the life-long journey of learning your special calling looks like. Yet the Clarity Spiral is the *first* master tool, not the last.

The second master tool is called the **Sweet Spot**. This master tool gathers multiple assessment instruments to reveal your greatest passions, your strongest abilities, and your ideal context. These coalesce into the One Thing that only you can do. The Sweet Spot master tool enables you to know and name your uniqueness.

The third master tool is called the **Vision Frame**. This master tool equips you to answer four big questions of life: "What am I here to do?" "Why am I doing it?" "How am I doing it?" "When am I successful?" The Vision Frame master tool enables you to know and name your identity.

The fourth master tool is called the **Horizon Storyline**. This master tool helps you answer the fifth big question of life: "Where is God taking me?" It projects your future into horizons of three years from now, one year from now, 90 days from now, and right now with increasing specificity, giving you practical and immediate steps to take in the plan God has for you. The Horizon

Storyline master tool enables you to know and name your direction.

The fifth and final master tool is called the **Life-Making Cycle**. This master tool institutes rhythms of review and renewal in your life at right-sized, regular intervals. The Life-Making Cycle enables you to move beyond knowing and naming your special calling to living it out every day.

I trust that the God who led Israel through the desert as a pillar of cloud and fire and who sustained his people with manna and water from the rock is leading and sustaining you by his Holy Spirit. Yet I also know that most of the time, God leads and sustains us through each other. I wrote this book and co-founded Younique to play my part in what God wants to do for us all—to enable us to know and name the good works he planned for us to do before the foundation of the world, and to walk in them.

More of Younique for More of You

If you want more of what Younique has to offer as you climb the mountain of clarity, you have several ways to access it.

First, you may belong to **a church where Younique is installed**. If so, take advantage of the great opportunities it provides you in the form of small groups, classes, weekend seminars, or retreats. Our heart's desire at Younique is that hundreds of thousands of people would experience the Younique Journey not by encountering any of us but by encountering Younique coaches at their local church.

The second option is to **contact Younique directly** at LifeYounique.com and register to walk the Younique Vision Journey with us. We have virtual cohorts that put you in a weekly small group with a coach using online conferencing. Alternatively, we have four-day accelerator events in cities across the country. You can also register for a two-day, one-on-one retreat with me (will@LifeYounique.com) or another Younique master trainer.

Finally, be on the lookout for **my forthcoming book** *Younique: Designing the Life God Dreamed for You*. This book provides a thorough introduction to the Younique Journey accompanied by rich teaching on personal calling and life design you won't find anywhere else. Go to the site YouniqueBook.com to sign up for free content before and after the book releases in January of 2020.

It's Your Call

I want to return to the words with which I started this chapter: "The single most important decision in your life is whether you believe that God is who he reveals he is. The second greatest decision is whether *you* will do what God made you to do."

As a fellow disciple of Jesus, I believe that you are indeed doing what God made you to do as much as you can. But I also suspect that, like many people, you're frustrated. You feel like there's something missing—like there's something more. Maybe you've gotten so discouraged that you've tried to convince yourself that things can't really be more satisfying in your life.

Take heart—more clarity is possible. God wants you to know yourself better in accordance with His knowledge of you. He's actually more invested in your success following your unique calling in life than you are—so invested that he paid his only Son to make it happen!

You are an unrepeatable creation. No one just like you has ever or will ever walk the face of this planet. You've climbed so much of the mountain already, but there's so much more to go. There are people and tools to help you get there, and with them at hand you can make it. It's never too late, you're never too old, and you've never failed too badly to climb higher up the peak of clarity. There's a life waiting to be lived that cannot be lived by anyone else.

So, are you ready to take the journey? It's your call.

ACKNOWLEDGMENTS

The greatest joy of all things Younique is a God-given, Olympic-quality core team.

I'm especially grateful to Younique Co-founder Dave Rhodes, who is the best disciple-making thinker and toolmaker I know. He is the chief master trainer at Younique and a true friend. The whole of the Younique Journey is our deep collaborative work. But where his original thought leadership and biblical insight are showcased I indicate with special attribution.

My collaborative writer, Cory Hartman, has been indispensable. He is a stellar thinker with a special gift for developing and expressing the key ideas of the Younique Journey in written form. He brought great encouragement as a friend, enthusiasm as a practitioner, and excellence as a fellow idea-artist.

As an organization, Younique would not exist without two special people. The first is Kelly Kannwischer, our current CEO. The second is Kandi Pfeiffer, who served as our startup executive director for the first two years. Both women have given sacrificially to make our organization a reality; I will be forever grateful.

Many thanks go to the wonderfully supportive team who provided amazing coordination and thoughtful feedback. Tessy McDaniel and Stefanie Drawdy always have my back with daily workflow. And a passionate team of volunteers made the final form of this book so much better. This group includes many initial readers from our first fifty certified coaches, with special contributions from Kelly Kannwischer, Kimber Liu, Luke Francis, David Bowman, and David Loveless.

Finally I am grateful to my wife Romy who graciously supports me when I take the time to put ideas on paper. She, along with my central circle, will forever be the guinea pigs of Younique tool development. I couldn't be me without you. Thank you Romy for expressing compassion, Dad for restoring integrity, Mom for lifting life, Jacob for activating growth, Joel for animating truth, Abby for simplifying connection, and Poema for . . . .

NOTES

[1] Os Guinness, *The Call: Finding and Fulfilling the Central Purpose of Your Life* (Nashville: Thomas Nelson, 2003), 30-31.

[2] One excellent exposition of this idea is Timothy Keller with Katherine Leary Alsdorf, *Every Good Endeavor: Connecting Your Work to God's Work* (New York: Dutton, 2012).

[3] Theology of Work Project, "Calling and Vocation: Overview," https://www.theologyofwork.org/key-topics/vocation-overview-article (accessed May 30, 2018).

[4] Ibid.

[5] Os Guinness, *The Call: Finding and Fulfilling the Central Purpose of Your Life* (Nashville: Thomas Nelson, 2003), 107.

[6] Timothy Ferriss and Arnold Schwarzenegger, *Tools of Titans: The Tactics, Routines, and Habits of Billionaires, Icons, and World-Class Performers* (New York: Houghton Mifflin Harcourt, 2017), 473.

[7] Parker Palmer, *Let Your Life Speak: Listening for the Voice of Vocation* (New York: Jossey-Bass, 1999), 5.

[8] I heard this phrase from a good friend, Brian McDougal, the executive pastor at Idlewild Baptist Church.

[9] Bill Burnett and Dave Evans, *Designing Your Life: How to Build a Well-Lived, Joyful Life,* (New York: Alfred A. Knopf, 2016), x.

[10] Damian Barr, *Get It Together: A Guide to Surviving your Quarterlife Crisis* (London: Hodder & Stoughton, 2004).

[11] Based on a Prosumer opinion survey of over 2,000 adults. Ashley Lutz, "See at What Age You Will Peak Physically, Mentally, Sexually, and Creatively," Business Insider,

http://www.businessinsider.com/age-for-peak-physical-mental-sexual-health-2012-7 (accessed July 30, 2018).

[12] Oswald Chambers, "Taking the Initiative Against Drudgery," *My Utmost for His Highest*, https://utmost.org/taking-the-initiative-against-drudgery (accessed June 13, 2018).

[13] This quote is variously attributed to William G. T. Shedd, John A. Shedd, and Grace Hopper.

[14] Garth Rosell, *The Surprising Work of God: Harold John Ockenga, Billy Graham, and the Rebirth of Evangelicalism* (Grand Rapids, MI: Baker Academic, 2008), 142.

[15] Timothy Ferriss and Arnold Schwarzenegger, *Tools of Titans: The Tactics, Routines, and Habits of Billionaires, Icons, and World-Class Performers* (New York: Houghton Mifflin Harcourt, 2017), 467-68.

YOUNIQUE

Learn more about the
Younique Experience
designed for the church
delivered through your church.

yourlifeyourcall.com

SLINGSHOT

GROUP

If you need my help
with coaching or staff search
you can find me here.

— Will Mancini

SlingshotGroup.org

auxanō®

Go Ahead

Create break-thru clarity as a
church team for visionary planning,
leadership pipeline and
capital campaigns.

---

auxano.com

Made in the USA
Columbia, SC
17 February 2019